WE WILL NOT BOW

TO BABYLON'S TABLE

A SPIRITUAL AND PRACTICAL COMPASS TO HELP OUR YOUTH NAVIGATE THROUGH A HOSTILE CULTURE

MICHAEL RACKLEY

We Will Not Bow to Babylon's Table

A Spiritual and Practical Compass to Help Our Youth Navigate through a Hostile Culture

by Michael Rackley

ISBN 13: 978-1-935986-57-7

P.O. Box 246295 Pembroke Pines, FL 33024
www.facebook.com/DrMichaelRackley
Email: rackleydeb@yahoo.com

LIBERTY
U N I V E R S I T Y.
PRESS
Lynchburg, Va.
www.Liberty.edu/LibertyUniversityPress

DEDICATION

The inspiration to write this book comes directly from the Lord of my life, Jesus Christ.

I would like to dedicate this book to my two daughters, Deborah and Anna, who motivated me to write this book because of their theological questions.

Also, to my wife Andrea who spent countless nights typing and encouraging me to finish what I started.

Lastly, to my students at the Miami Job Corps Center and to young people all over the world who faithfully came to Bible study for the past seventeen years, despite their wounds, brokenness, and discouragement, and allowed Christ to transform them.

DISCLAIMER

The purpose of this book is to encourage young people to be like Christ and to stand strong against the evils of this world. This book does not make the claim to have all of the answers to young people problems, yet it is meant to point to One who does — Jesus Christ our Lord. This book is aimed to encourage, correct, teach, coach, and motivate youth to live out their faith in a manner that's pleasing to the Lord. The author declares that to the best of his knowledge all material (quoted or not) contained herein is accurate; and we shall not be held liable for the same.

TABLE OF CONTENTS

PREFACE

We Will Not Bow to Babylon's Table is a thrilling exposition about four godly teenagers — Hananiah (Shadrach), Mishael (Meshach), Azariah (Abed-nego), and Daniel (Belteshazzar) — living in a heathen society. These teens believed God and refused to compromise by bowing to Babylon's Table (the world). This book has the potential to change the lives of young people, parents, college students, children, at-risk youth, and future generations by providing answers to many of their questions.

Because I have witnessed the self-destructive behavior of young people all over the world, I wrote this commentary on the first chapter of the Book of Daniel.

During my ten years as a pastor, seventeen years as a Bible study teacher at the Miami Job Corps Center, and twenty years as an educator, I have ministered to at-risk youths from various ethnic backgrounds. These groups include Hispanic, African-American, Caucasian, Jamaican, Haitian, Bahamian, Cuban, Mexican, Puerto Rican, and others. I have also counseled and taught biblical studies to young people of different religious denominations, cults, and other groups, such as Jehovah's Witnesses, Islam, Santeria, Rastafarianism, Alien Occultism, Ouija Board users, drug addicts, satanism, skin heads, Catholicism, Mormonism, voodooism, Crypts, Bloods, Latin Kings, atheism, witches, warlocks, homosexuals, Hebrew occults, inner-city gang members, Seventh Day Adventists, incest victims, and more. Through my experiences in counseling and teaching, I have found that they all have one thing in common: there is a void, a hidden and deep longing for something greater than themselves. Only Christ Jesus, our Lord, can satisfy this longing.

By examining apocalyptic literature with a modern-day contemporary view, this book unmasks the diabolical plan of both Satan and the world against our young people. In this challenging book, I aim to help you discover the truths about issues that go unanswered in many communities. As you read this information, I will reveal Satan's attempt to change your true identity with his world table of delicacies. You will learn how to take a holy stand against the ways of this world, eat healthy, experience God's favor and tender love, and gain God-given knowledge and skills that you can to publicly display in Jesus' name.

ACKNOWLEDGMENTS

I wish to thank my mother Mercy De Jones, my father
Sherman Rackley, my family, and my Lord and Savior Jesus Christ.
They raised me, supported me, taught me, and loved me.

INTRODUCTION

There is a giant in the land with a Herculean-like spiritual force opposing Christ and His Church, walking the Earth, and speaking blasphemous words of idolatry. In his arsenal are cults, sects, entertainers, athletes, corporations, media conglomerates, countries, universities, actors, musicians, school boards, political parties, secret societies, and apostate churches. His dark army, Babylon as we know it, has been birthed from Hell itself. It is led by the deceiver, Satan, and his evil hordes that employ false religions, illegal drugs, gangs, violence, murder, fornication, lies, authoritarian governments, and wickedness in high places. He has lured many to the corridors of Hell.

But there is a beam of light that invades darkness: A Champion, a Rock (Stone). The prophet Daniel reveals: "The stone was cut out of the mountain without hands, and that it break in pieces" and consumes all kingdoms, and it shall stand forever. (Daniel 2:45 KJV Full Life Study Bible) Who is this Rock? Jesus Christ, the one and only conquering Messiah, Eternal King, Ancient of Days, the Lord of Glory, King of Kings, Lord of Lords, who is known as Christ Jesus, our Lord.

Christ has secret weapons! The Church has neglected it; most pastors have forgotten about it; many parents have abandoned it. These weapons were birthed from the womb of the Almighty God. It is our youth — teenagers and young adults. Islam uses them successfully because it expects young people to live and to die for their faith. On the other hand, the Christian Church expects attendance and little else from their youth members. When did the Church stop depending on young people? When did the church stop trusting in God for its young people? It is simple. The Church stopped relying on God as its source for the youth and started to believe it knew all of the answers.

The characters in this book are four godly teens, some haters, the wicked King Nebuchadnezzar, and an Awesome God.

The word "Babylon" is translated from the Hebrew word "Babel" which means "confusion" (Gen. 11:1-9). According to history, the Babylonian name has endured some changes throughout time: "The Babylonian name as it stood in the first millennium B.C. had been changed from an earlier Babilli in early second millennium B.C., possibly meaning *Gate of God* or *Gateway of the Gods*."[1] In this next section we enter Babylon's past and future through the books of Daniel and Revelation from which this commentary is based on.

PAST

Ancient City of Babylon — Where is its geographical location?

According to history, the ancient city of Babylon was located about 50 miles south of modern Baghdad in Iraq, between the Euphrates and Tigris Rivers.

Ancient City of Babylon — Description

According to the website www.bible-history.com/babylonia[2] the historian Herodotus (BK1, 178-186) describes King Nebuchadnezzar's Babylon with the following attributes:

- It was in the form of a square, 14 miles on each side, and of enormous magnitude.
- It boasted a brick wall that was 56 miles long, 300 feet high, and 25 feet thick with another wall 75 feet behind the first one, and the second wall extended 35 feet below the ground.
- A wide and deep moat surrounded the city.
- It had 250 towers that were each 450 feet high.
- The Euphrates River flowed through the middle of the city. Ferry boats were used on the river. A half mile long drawbridge closed at night.
- It encompassed the Hanging Gardens (one of the wonders of

---

1 http://www.bible-history.com/babylonia
2 Ibid.

the ancient world). Water was raised from the river by hydraulic pumps to keep the plants hydrated.

- There were 8 massive gates that lead to the inner city and one hundred brass gates.
- The streets were paved with stone slabs.
- It possessed the Great Tower (a ziggurat) and 53 temples including the Great Temple of Marduk." There were 180 altars erected to the goddess Ishtar.
- The golden image of Baal and the Golden Table (both weighing over 500,000 lbs and made of solid gold) were within the city walls.
- There were 2 golden lions and a solid gold human figure measuring 18 feet high
- King Nebuchadnezzar's palace was considered, at the time, to be the most magnificent building ever erected on Earth.

Ancient City of Babylon — Who did the people worship?

Babylon has a polytheistic culture, meaning they worshiped more than one god. Actually, the people worshiped hundreds of gods. For example, they worshiped the god of the elements, love, war, wisdom, the moon, and the sun.

Ancient City of Babylon — What was their culture?

"The most famous innovation of the ancient Babylonian culture was astronomy, which began as the study of astrology."[3] Babylonians were the first to create what we know as horoscopes. The Bible strictly forbids this practice which will be addressed in a later chapter.

Ancient City of Babylon — More Information

King Nebuchadnezzar, ruler of Babylon, was known for his military might, his hanging gardens, his empire's splendor, and, lastly, his destruction of Jerusalem.

---

3   http://www.allaboutHistory.org

FUTURE

Future of Babylon — Revelation 17-18

"The mother of harlots and abominations of the Earth" is used symbolically for Babylon in Revelation 17 to represent a counterfeit religious system mixed with paganism and doctrines of the Christian faith. The literal city of Babylon will be rebuilt in the end times with its false world religions and ideologies that deceive people through astrology, witchcraft, political power, prestige, secrecy, wealth, and its anti-Israel and anti-Church rhetoric which seems to fit in the seven year tribulation before Christ second advent. Judgment is pronounced against this city, "Babylon the Great is fallen, is fallen, and is become the habitation of devils, and the hold of every foul spirit, and a cage of every unclean and hateful bird." (Revelation 18:2 KJV Full Life Study Bible). Following this judgment is a prophetic call to repentance, "Come out of her, my people, that ye receive not of her plagues. For her sins have reached unto Heaven, and God has remembered her iniquities." (18:4 KJV Full Life Study Bible) Believers are instructed to flee this city, and escape the final verdict of God on it. Christians must stand for Christ in word and in deed. The Apostle Paul told young Timothy, "Thou therefore endure hardness as a good soldier of Jesus Christ. No man that wareth entangles himself with the affairs of this life, that he may please Him who have chosen him to be a soldier." (II Timothy 2:3-4 KJV Full Life Study Bible). Believers should seek to follow these words of truth.

Babylon Today

In our modern day society we have around us Babylonian astrology (zodiac signs/horoscopes), false religious systems, many camouflage forms of idolatry, political power, consumerism, humanism, materialism, lust, a postmodern worldview, new age movement, atheism, adultery, and much more. Today, this culture is hostile to the family, marriage between one natural born man and one natural born woman, the Biblical Christian Worldview, absolute truth, and the Bible.

There are many that believe that Babylon in Revelation 17 and 18 is America, but this is far from the truth based on the grammatical-historical literal interpretation of the Bible consistently and Old Testament prophesies about Babylon. Although, America is declining morally and biblically from the truth, according to scripture America isn't mentioned. We must remember that God doesn't have a covenant with America, but He has covenants with Israel and the Church.

Babylon in Daniel chapter one is a place in your life you thought you would never be. "Babylon is where you find yourself when life does not turn out the way you planned it."[4] The evidences of living in a Babylonian society are presented in these scenarios:

A young girl who's pressured to have sex, a teenage boy/girl being bullied, a young man angry at the world because his parents are getting a divorce, Christian in a hostile environment, a high school student's faith is being challenge by his/her teacher, an adolescent addicted to drugs, a college student is pressured to have sex because of peer pressure, students don't believe Jesus rose from the dead, youth group is fun, but not challenging, teenager harassed by gangs daily to join, teen age drop out, and teens facing crises after crises and need help.

"You find yourself in Babylon, cut off from the life that you wanted and planned on, and you may never get home (like Daniel and friends). And worst of all, you wonder if God even cares. You may ask questions like: How could God let this happen? Has He forgotten His promise? Does He even notice? What do you do when you find yourself, like Daniel, in Babylon?"[5]

---

4   http://www.cc-vw.org/sermons/daniel.htm
5   Ibid.

CHAPTER 1

THE DIABOLICAL PLAN OF SATAN FOR OUR YOUTH IS TO STEAL, TO KILL, AND TO DESTROY

The Bible is the inspired, inerrant, and infallible Word of God. Chapter one of the Book of Daniel will be used as our guide and standard for living holy in a modern-day society for the young people of tomorrow. Daniel's personal dedication to God is an example to the exiles as well as our young people on how they should live in a modern-day Babylonian society.

"Jesus says, 'I am the Door; anyone who enters in through me will be saved (will live). He will come in and he will go out [freely], and will find pasture. The thief comes only in order to steal and kill and destroy. I came that they may have and enjoy life and have it in abundance (to the full, until it overflows)'" (AMP, John 10:9-10).

> **COOL FACT**
>
> *Did you know that the Old Testament was originally written in Hebrew and the New Testament in Greek?*

Before we follow Daniel and his teenage friends into Babylon, I will briefly give you some staggering statistics from Josh McDowell's book, *The Last Christian Generation,* in which Satan's diabolical plan is unveiled against our young people.

For starters:

- 63% don't believe Jesus is the Son of the One True God
- 58% believe all faiths teach equally valid truths
- 51% don't believe Jesus rose from the dead
- 65% don't believe Satan is a real entity
- 68% don't believe the Holy Spirit is a real entity[1]

---

1   Barna Research Group, "Third Millennium Teens" (Ventura, CA: The Barna Research Group, Ltd., (1999), 51.

Just as a reminder, these statistics come from church youths! These young people are faithfully attending church services with their parents, grandparents, and guardians and they are surrendering their faith in Christ, to adopting a post-modern way of life in our presence.

David says, "… If the foundations are destroyed, what can the [unyieldingly] righteous do, or what has He [the Righteous One] wrought or accomplished" (AMP, Psalms 11:3)? It is here the Scripture reveals that if there is no foundation, there is no belief system, there is no hope, and the consequences are revealed in these statistics.

> **COOL FACT**
>
> *"Apologia" is Greek for "ready defense" (AMP, 1 Peter 3:15)*

"Research shows that when young people lack a basic biblical belief system, it negatively affects their attitudes. As a result they are:"

- 225% are more likely to be angry with life
- 216% are more likely to be resentful
- 210% are more likely to lack purpose in life
- 200% are more likely to be disappointed in life[2]

"The research also shows that our young people's failure to adopt a foundational Christian belief system negatively impacts their behavior:"

- 48% are more likely to cheat on an exam
- 200% are more likely to steal
- 200% are more likely to physically hurt someone
- 300% are more likely to use illegal drugs
- 600% more likely to attempt suicide[3]

These behavioral statistics give us a glimpse of how Satan's diabolical plan is to steal, to kill, and to destroy our youth. Fear not brothers and sisters, Jesus says, "I came that they may have and enjoy life and have it in abundance (to the full, until it overflows)."

As we accompany the teenagers Daniel and friends into Babylon, the evil plan of King Nebuchadnezzar unfolds.

---

2   Ibid., 65.

3   Ibid., 43.

In the third year of the reign of Jehoiakim king of Judah, Nebuchadnezzar king of Babylon came to Jerusalem and besieged it. And the Lord delivered Jehoiakim king of Judah into his hand, along with some of the articles from the temple of God. These he carried off to the temple of his god in Babylonia and put in the treasure house of his god. (NIV, Daniel 1:1-2)

Remember that the previous scripture reveals that God uses Babylon as an instrument of divine judgment against Israel.

> **COOL FACT**
>
> *In 1948 the state of Israel was established. The country is about the size of New Jersey.*

This new and foreign surrounding brought Daniel to crossroads in his life. History reveals that Babylon was the center of idol worship and idolatrous religions, but Daniel knew he had been powerless to stop his deportation to this wicked place. He also knew that he could only be defiled by his own actions. This was the decisive test for Daniel and his friends, and it was not an easy one to pass. After all, he had been taken into captivity not because of his own sins, but because of his father's sin of disobeying the Word of God. The Jewish people were carried into captivity because they chose to embrace idolatry and were negligent in the worship of Yahweh, the True God.

It is here we see similarities with today's youth born into environments that are beyond their control. Examples of these environments include single family households, poverty-stricken, dysfunctional, violent neighborhoods that are drug infested. These environments are swarmed with neighborhood gangs forcing new memberships at early ages; they are also contaminated with disease, hopelessness, homelessness,

> **COOL FACT**
>
> *Did you know "peace" in Hebrew means "Shalom." It means "happy, well, prosperity, protected, and debt free."*

absent parents, and illegitimacy. On the other hand, some young people are born into middle and upper class environments but they are forced in the same situation because of their family's rejection of God. The absence of God summons spiritual darkness and both groups of people are subject to satanic attacks as a result of this.

Many of our young people are asking questions within themselves in these environments. Questions like, Does anyone see me? Can anyone help me? I'm afraid! I don't know which way to go or what to do? Community leaders are scrambling for answers. Parents are bewildered. Law enforcement agencies are trying to come together for answers with little or no success. The church presence in many cases is of little affect. The answer to this struggle is found in the pages of scripture. Jesus says, "I am the Way and the Truth and the Life; no one comes to the Father except (through) Me" (AMP, John 14:6). It is in this scripture that God in the Flesh (Jesus Christ) reveals and answers the three greatest questions of the human spirit.

How can someone like me be saved?

How can I be certain?

How can I be satisfied?

---

(1) How can someone like me be saved?

Jesus answers, "I am the Way." In order to answer this question, one must admit to being lost and spiritually bankrupt. When you know Christ, you know the Way because He is the Way. There are numerous ways to come to Jesus, but there is only one way to get to Heaven...by Him (Christ).

(2) How can I be certain?

Jesus answered, "I am the Truth." Jesus not only taught the truth, but taught that He is the truth. The absolute truth is not found in philosophy, religion, music, knowledge, or in crystal balls. The absolute truth is found in Christ alone.

(3) How can I be satisfied?

Jesus answered, "I am the Life." The word life is Zoe [ζωή] in the Greek means fulfillment, contentment, peace, joy, security, deliverance, healing, peace of mind, and the heart's ease. This life is revealed in the person of Jesus Christ and only comes to a man by trusting in Jesus Christ. Evidence of the Zoë [ζωή] kind of life is explained in the Book of Galatians which is the fruits of the spirit: Love, joy, peace, patience, kindness, goodness, gentleness, and self-control (5:22-23). These qualities are the results of a fulfilled life in Christ.

> **COOL FACT**
>
> *During the time of Jesus, the Jewish people also spoke Aramaic & a Semite language used for that time possibly dating back from 70 years exile in Babylon during the time of Daniel.*

THE EVIL PLAN OF KING NEBUCHADNEZZAR

"And the [Babylonian] king told Ashpenaz, the master of his eunuchs, to bring in some of the children of Israel, both of the royal family and of the nobility" (AMP, Daniel 1:3).

What was this evil plan of King Nebuchadnezzar? "And the King told Ashpenaz, the master of his eunuchs, to bring in some of the children of Israel, both of the Royal Family and of the nobility." From this verse in the Book of Daniel, it is clear that King Nebuchadnezzar had designed a plan whereby the most promising of his captives should serve him. The children mentioned in the preceding scripture weren't babies, but were teenagers and were the finest that Israel had to offer. In today's churches, schools, and all around our nation we still have young people like Daniel and friends who the devil try to stalk and prey upon tenaciously because of their talents and gifts, their keen minds, physical appearances, athletic abilities, and potential in Christ. The gifts that I am referring to don't exclude ministry callings like pastors, bishops, prophets, and even as parents to name a few.

> **COOL FACT**
>
> *Jerusalem is called the City of Peace, the Holy Land, and the Holy City of the Prophets*

Gifts from the Lord make an individual different. This is why, Child of God, you don't fit-in with worldly crowds — you are not better but you are peculiar and different. You even think and act differently. In reads, "For you are bought with a price: therefore glorify God in your body, and in your spirit, which are God's." (*KJV, 1 Corinthians 6:20*). Is it by accident that most of the secular artists have a church background? The talents and gifts you possess are God given; don't prostitute your gift to the world, but glorify God through and with your gifts. Jesus says, "For what will profit a man if he gains the whole world and forfeits his life [his blessed life in the Kingdom of God]? Or what would a man give as an exchange for his [blessed] life [in the Kingdom of God]?" (AMP, Matthew 16:26)

The Kingdom of Darkness is a highway to hell that leads to destruction. On this attractive highway there are many people and many signs: yield right of way to drugs, violence, murder, stealing, skipping school, pre-marital sex, false religions, and the occult. On this road, there is no real happiness. Jesus states, "Enter through the narrow gate; for wide is the gate and spacious and broad is the way that leads away to destruction, and many are those who are entering through it. But the gate is narrow and the way is straightened and compressed that leads away to life, few are those who find it" (AMP, Matthew 7:13). This narrow gate is the gate that leads to heaven. On this narrow road is no guarantee of becoming a millionaire, but God promises to fulfill our needs according to His riches in glory in Christ Jesus. On this road there is no guarantee we won't have bumps, bruises or scrapes, but there is a promise of a smooth landing. Few travel on this road but Jesus says, "I'll never leave you nor forsake you." On the narrow road, man is God-conscious; however, on the broad road man is sin-conscious. On the narrow road, one has a spiritual family, bond, and friendship that lasts a lifetime.

Brothers and sisters there are two roads — the road that leads from earth to heaven, and the road that leads from earth to hell. Choose you this day who you will serve. Don't give up! In Jesus' name, you will make it. Hold on to His unchanging hand. I dare you to be like Daniel and his friends.

PURPOSE

Have you ever wondered why the Lord would many times refer to us as "children," or why He uses children in the Bible as you will see in later chapters for His glory? This is simply because God wants us to be like dear little children in the Kingdom because children have no sense of limitation in Him. They don't know about failure. "Remember, the body has to be taught failure. That's why children don't know that things are impossible. They know no limits. Spirit has no limits, which is what we must re-learn as adults. The power of single-minded purpose and focused imagination is everything. If you move into unity in your thoughts, nothing can stop the outcome."[4]

DISCUSSION QUESTIONS

1. What is the diabolical plan of Satan? Where is the scripture found?
2. What are the three greatest questions of the human spirit?
3. According to the numbers, what percentages of young people don't believe in Jesus as the Son of God?
4. What are the results of not having a basic biblical belief system?
5. What is the ζωή Zoe kind of life?
6. What does apologia means in reference to 1 Peter 3:15?

---

4   E. Bernard Jordan, *The Laws of Thinking* (USA: Hay House, 2006), 186

NOTES

_____

_____

_____

_____

_____

_____

_____

_____

_____

_____

_____

_____

_____

_____

_____

_____

_____

_____

_____

CHAPTER 2

THE VIRGIN

"Young men without any physical defect (blemish), handsome, showing aptitude for every kind of learning, well informed, quick to understand, and qualified to serve in the king's palace He was to teach them the language and literature of the Babylonians" (NIV, Daniel 1:4).

In Daniel 1:4 we see two worldviews clashing in Babylon. Daniel and friends were Hebrews from Israel that believed and served the One True and Living God, Yahweh. They were held as captives in a hostile land and they held a monotheistic belief system. Monotheism is the belief that there is one God; this conviction is established in Judaism, Christianity and Islam. Babylon was a Polytheistic empire that worshiped more than one god or deity. Today there are many opposing worldviews in America, but our focus will be on Christianity in a post-modern world. Post-modernity, "involves radical change, especially from what has been accepted as morally, ethically, and spiritually correct in the world."[1] Christianity is the belief that Jesus Christ is the Son of God born of a virgin, fully man, fully God and recognizes salvation is in the person of Jesus as accomplished in His crucified death, burial, and resurrection. Jesus' substitutionary death for the forgiveness of sins, the Trinity, the authority of the Bible, Second Coming and being Savior of the world is also proof of our salvation and our belief system.

---

1   Henry Blackaby, *Postmodernism: Is It a Fad or Here to Stay?* On Mission, September-October 2002, 16

Figure A.

Major Religions	Monotheistic	Doctrine
Christianity	Believe in one God, infinite Spirit, creator, and sustainer of all things, who exists eternally in three persons, God the Father, God the Son (Jesus Christ), and God the Holy Spirit. These three are one in essence but distinct in person and function.	Holy Bible, consisting of the Old and New Testament
Judaism	Believe there is only One God, known as (Yahweh)	Torah, including mainly the Old Testament
Islam	Believe in only one god (Allah)	Qur'an

Believing right is wrong and wrong is right is a fulfillment of Scripture. The Apostle Paul reveals: "In whom the god of this world hath blinded the minds of them which believe not, lest the light of the glorious gospel of Christ, who is the image of God should shine unto them" (KJV, II Corinthians 4:4). This verse confirms, metaphorically speaking, how many of our young people minds have been blinded — meaning their thinking have been clouded due to a post-modern culture.

The majority of young people hear about Christ, but they do not personally know Him nor do they grasp His claims of divinity. The biblical character Job had a similar condition. Job reflects on the circumstances that he has just been through, "I had heard of you [only] by the hearing of the ear, but now my [spiritual] eye sees You" (AMP, Job 42:5). Job is saying, I really know you now (after my trials, after my children dying, after my disease, and after my friends turned their backs on me) as Lord, Creator, physician, and miracle worker. In other words, he is saying to God: I have spent time with you, and in that experienced, I found you to be a faithful and an awesome Lord.

Figure B[2]

Word	Christian Understanding *(Youth Culture)*	Postmodern Understanding *(Youth Culture)*
Personal Preference	Personal Preferences with Biblical Parameters.	Preferences of sexual behaviors and value systems are personally determined.
Personal Rights	Everyone has the right to be treated justly under the law.	Everyone has the right to do whatever he or she believes is best for him or herself.
Freedom	Being free to do what's right to do according to a Christian Biblical Worldview.	Being able to do anything you want to do.
Truth	Absolute Truth is not subject to change, nor man's opinion.	Whatever is right for you.

THE ASSAULT ON VIRGINS

In the Hebrew dictionary, the word "blemish" (מוּאָם) means "to stain (physically or morally), blot, and spot." Daniel and his friends were likely between the ages of 12-17, they were morally righteous, and they were literally virgins — people who have not engaged in sexual intercourse or sexual activities. They were also scripturally versed because they studied the Bible. In addition, they intellectually knew God, spiritually prayed to him, and personally had a relationship with Him despite being separated from their parents and godly influence. These teenagers, Daniel and his friends, are perfect role models for young people today who refuse to be violated spiritually, emotionally, intellectually, and physically because they had an intimate relationship with God based on scripture.

This leads me to ask the question: Why does Satan and the world seek virgins today? According to the Book of John, Satan wants to steal, kill, and destroy everything (10: 10). The word *"steal"* in the Greek is *"klepto* (κλέψη)"* meaning "to take away by theft." The enemy wants to steal

---

2   Josh McDowell and David H. Bellis, *The Last Christian Generation* (Holiday, Florida: Green Key Books, 2006), 23.

every person's innocence, dreams, ideas, womanhood, and manhood as well as the sanctity of marriage. He wants to steal your testimony and put another notch on his belt, giving him bragging rights. I have counseled many single young ladies who have had their virginity stolen from them with or without their consent. They carry much shame and regret about it. In college, there are many upperclassmen seeking freshman—aka "freshmeat." It is assumed that all freshman are vulnerable and naïve. As a result of this thinking, upperclassmen gamble to see which of them can have sex with these underclassmen first. What a tragedy! Young people are leaving home as virgins and returning home cheated by the allure of the sexually experienced. Sexually transmitted infections and other consequences can come along with the deception and with the premarital sex experience. These young people are confused because many parents did not arm them with a Christian Biblical Worldview and a solid relationship with Christ, so they could be victorious in the University of Babylon.

There are many weapons that the enemy has in his arsenal against the children of God. One of the many weapons used by the enemy of your faith is secular romance novels. The world is using these captivating sexual love stories that are pornographic in nature. They are aimed at arousing our youth's sexual appetite and curiosity at an early age. These are tactical attacks from the world that I like to call "home invaders" because our youth are bringing these books into their private quarters. Many parents are ignorant of what their children are reading and what they are carrying around in their bags, thus allowing the enemy to come in and steal their children's innocence.

Parents, if you do not allow strangers to walk through your door, why do you allow them to come in through your televisions, computers, magazines, and books? Parents often have an alarm for the home and a dog in their yards for physical protection, but what about spiritual, moral, and emotional protection? Just like you have locks on your doors, you need a safeguard system in place for these outsiders. Many parents are praying. Great! However, communicating with your children is still very important because you are their first line of defense. The Book of

Proverbs says, "Train up a child in the way he should go: and when he is old, he will not depart from it" (KJV, 22:6). *You have a greater influence than anyone else.*

BORN-AGAIN VIRGINS

"The thief comes only in order to steal and kill and destroy" (AMP, John 10:10a)

Many believers have lost their virginity and innocence. For some, it happened as a form of sexual abuse beyond their control. For others, it may have been a choice out of ignorance or pressure, resulting in bondage to sin, shame, guilt, and regret. Despite this sad fact, the Word of God provides some good news. In the Book of John Jesus says, "I came that they may have and enjoy life, and have it in abundance [to the full, until it overflows]" (AMP, 10:10).

TEMPTATION

What should you do if you are tempted to have sex? The Apostle Paul advises believers to "Flee also youthful lusts: but follow righteousness, faith, charity, peace, with them that call on the Lord out of a pure heart" (KJV, II Timothy 2:22). "Youthful lusts" have devastated the lives of teens and young adults, have destroyed marriages, produced unwanted pregnancies, and even caused many to lose their lives. The Greek verb for *"flee"* is "pheugo (φευγε)" which is a second person, singular, present, active, imperative verb that means to literally "run away or escape as fast and as far as you can." In other words, believers need to physically avoid places, people, events, and situations that can lead to reckless behavior. Paul commands followers to continue to flee youthful lusts (**over and over again**) in the present The reason the believer is to flee over and over is because "flee" is also a Greek present tense verb as a mentioned earlier, rendering action

> ## BORN-AGAIN VIRGINS
> *Are believers that have engaged in sex before marriage, but rededicates himself/herself to God.*

COOL FACTS

Who would have thought to have found adultery in David, and drunkenness in Noah, and cursing in Job? If god leaves a man to himself, how suddenly and scandalously may sin break forth in the holiest man in the earth! "I say unto all, Watch." A wandering heart needs a watchful eye. ~Thomas Watson

happening continuously in the present. This means the believers must continually remain on guard in their Christian walk and "fight the good fight of faith."

Paul reminds believers of the consequences of defiance of God's Word:

"Do you not know that the unrighteous and the wrongdoers will not inherit or have any share in the Kingdom of God? Do not be deceived (mislead): neither the impure and immoral, nor idolaters, not adulterers, nor those who participate in homosexuality. Nor cheats (swindlers and thieves), nor greedy graspers, nor drunkards, nor foulmouthed revilers and slanderers, nor extortioners and robbers will not inherit or have any share in the Kingdom of God" (AMP, 1 Corinthians 6:9-10).

Falling into temptation is like kryptonite to the Christian believer; it zaps the power of God in your life and leaves you powerless and weak in your spiritual walk. Be encouraged, there is power when you follow Scripture, make wise decisions, reject temptation, and embrace purity, holiness, and righteousness.

DENUNCIATION OF SEXUAL SINS

If you are struggling with sexual sin, it comes a point in time when you must by faith make a declaration to God and denounce your sexual sin by first saying, "I am tired of being a slave to this sin, I am tired of being tired and I am tired of feeling hopeless." Proceed with this prayer:

"Almighty God, I have come to you in the name of Jesus Christ our Lord. He is God in the flesh, the Lamb of God that takes away the sins of the world for all of those who repent, trust, believe, and confess Him as Lord. The precious blood of Jesus cleanses me from all sin and damnation. I am free from all contamination of sexual nature through my five senses and direct participation in sin. I vow based on your word to a life a purity and commitment to change and to follow you. Your Word declares in (AMP, Micah 7:18-19)—"Who is a God like you, who forgives iniquity and passes over the transgression of the remnant of His heritage? He retains not his anger forever, because He delights in mercy and loving kindness. He will again have compassion on us; He will subdue and tread underfoot our iniquities. You will cast all our sins into the depths of the sea."

I believe your Word and I pray all these things in Jesus' name. Amen."

COOL FACTS

Did you know eunuchs had to be castrated in order to serve in the palace of Babylon? (Daniel 1:3)

Remember, God is a God of another chance. Now that you have denounced your sin, prayed the prayer of faith, and confessed Christ as your Lord and Savior, you are now a born again virgin! Now locate a Bible-believing church in your neighborhood and live for Christ.

Did you know that the Bible points out more than one sexual sin? The New Testament uses four ways to describe fornication (premarital sex and extramarital sex):

- Voluntary sexual intercourse of an unmarried person with someone of the opposite sex(1 Corinthians 7:2; 1 Thessalonians 4:3)
- Adultery (Matthew 5:32, 19:9)
- Harlotry and prostitution (Revelation 2:14, 20)
- Various forms of unchasity (John 8:41; Acts 15:20; 1 Corinthians 5:1)[3]

These four descriptions of fornication can keep believers informed that they can guard their bodies to remain pure. "...Within the boundary of marriage, sex is for procreation of children, enhancement of the one-flesh relationship, and enjoyment for married couples whose love can be nourished thereby. Outside of the limits established by God, sex can quickly become an evil and destructive force in human life. Marital sexual

---

3   Trent C. Butler, ed. *Holman Bible Dictionary* (Nashville, TN: Holman Bible Publishers, 1991), 511.

love is both a gift and a responsibility from God to be consecrated by the Word and prayer."[4]

50 REASONS YOU'RE NOT READY TO HAVE SEX

Count the cost and ask yourself if you are ready to go all the way? Consider your ways, but remember that Christ is your first love and that sex is for marriage. Your body is not for recreational sexual activity, sexually transmitted diseases, or unplanned pregnancy outside of marriage. Your body is the Temple of the Holy Spirit.

Here is a list of fifty reasons outlined by Sean Covey, author of *The 7 Habits of Highly Effective Teens*, on why you are not prepared to have sex before marriage:[5]

1. You think sex equals love.
2. You feel pressured.
3. You are afraid to say no.
4. It is just easier to give in.
5. You think everyone else is doing it. (They're not!)
6. Your instincts tell you not to.
7. You don't know the facts about pregnancy.
8. You don't understand how birth control works.
9. You don't think a woman can get pregnant the first time. (She can.)
10. It goes against your moral beliefs.
11. It goes against your religious beliefs.
12. You will regret it in the morning.
13. You will feel embarrassed or ashamed.
14. You are doing it to prove something.
15. You cannot support a child.
16. You cannot support yourself.
17. Your idea of commitment is a 3-day video rental.

---

4   Ibid.

5   Excerpts from *You're Not Ready to Have Sex If...*Copyright 1996 Journeyworks Publishing, Santa Cruz, CA. Reprinted with permission.

18. You believe sex before marriage is wrong.

19. You don't know how to protect yourself from HIV—the virus that causes AIDS.

20. You don't know the signs and symptoms of sexually transmitted infections (STI's, also called STD's).

21. You think it will make your partner love you.

22. You think it will make you love your partner.

23. You think it will keep you and your partner together.

24. You hope it will change your life.

25. You don't want it to change your life.

26. You are not ready for the relationship to change.

27. You are drunk.

28. You wish you were drunk.

29. Your partner is drunk.

30. You expect it to be perfect.

31. You will just die if it's not perfect.

32. You cannot laugh together about awkward elbows and clumsy clothes.

33. You are not ready to take off your clothes.

34. You think HIV and AIDS only happen to other people.

35. You think you can tell who has HIV by looking at them.

36. You don't think teens get HIV. (They do.)

37. You don't know that abstinence is the only 100% protection against sexually transmitted infections and pregnancy.

38. You have not talked about tomorrow.

39. You cannot face the thought of tomorrow.

40. You would be horrified if your parents found out.

41. You are doing it just so your parents will find out.

42. You are too scared to think clearly.

43. You think it will make you more popular.

44. You think you owe it to your partner.

45. You think it's not OK to be a virgin.

46. You are only thinking about yourself.

47. You are not thinking about yourself.

48. You cannot wait to tell everyone about it.

49. You hope no one would hear about it.

50. You really wish the whole thing had never come up.

Now that you have made the right decisions to not have sex before the wedding, know that it is okay to wait until marriage.

DISCUSSION QUESTIONS

1. What is post-modernism?
    a. What is the difference between the post-modern and the Christian worldview concerning values?
2. What is a virgin?
3. What is a born-again virgin?
4. Is it a sin to be tempted?
5. What is the purpose of sexuality within the boundaries of marriage?
6. Is sex before marriage really a sin?
    a. Use scriptural verses to support your answer.
    b. List 10 reasons you are not ready to have sex before marriage.
7. Discuss the benefits of waiting to have sex until you are married.

NOTES

CHAPTER 3

TALENTS AND GIFTS

"Young men without any physical defect, handsome, showing aptitude for every kind of learning, well informed, quick to understand, and qualified to serve in the king's palace. He was to teach them the language and literature of the Babylonians" (*NIV, Daniel 1:4*).

Webster's Dictionary defines talent as *an aptitude or ability of a person.* The word gift is defined as *something that is given from one person to another.* The good news is that everyone has a spiritual gift or a talent that can be used to change the world around them, thus being possible world changers.

This leads me to ask the question, What was it that attracted King Nebuchadnezzar to the children of Israel — their talents and gifts? Scripture reveals that Daniel and his friends' talents were skills in all wisdom, cunning knowledge, and understanding of science. Every man, woman, and child saved or unsaved has gifts and talents given to them by the Lord. The Apostle Paul reminds believers, "For the gifts and calling of God are without repentance" (*KJV*, Romans 11:29). Jesus tells of the parable of talents, "And unto one he gave five talents, to another two, and to another one; to every man according to his several abilities; and straightway took his journey" (*KJV*, Matthew 25:14-15). The gifts that God has given you is meant to be used for His glory that the light of Christ within us will shine bright for the world to see.

WHAT IS YOUR TALENT OR GIFT?

Most people are asking the age old question, what's my talent or gift? Well, my question to them would be — what is it that you hate or love the most? Talents are skills, gifts, time, and resources that can be used in living for Christ. I've found through experience, trial, and error that exposure is the key that unlocks the door to a world of opportunities. Generally lawyers study law because they hate injustice; doctors study medicine because they hate seeing sick people; policemen swear to protect and serve because they hate seeing people defenseless. In many cases family, coworkers, or friends have already mentioned what they thought you were gifted in, but we reject it by either comparing ourselves to someone else or through underestimation. "A man's gift maketh room for him, and bringeth him before great men." (KJV, Proverbs 18:16). Once you discover your gifts and talents, it is your responsibility to cultivate and polish that gift (i.e. taking online courses or even obtaining a degree). Consultation from someone who believes in your dream and who is willing to take that step of faith with you is a good start. Work at the vision until it comes to pass. One word to sum up my explanation is exposure. As an educator I tell my students that it's difficult to visualize going to college in another state, when you haven't been across the street or in the next county in your community. Universities understand this concept well and this is why they arrange college tours to acclimate students to their new environment. Remember what the Book of Proverbs advises, "And in an abundance of counselors there is victory and safety" (24:6b). In other words, seek exposure and the advice of mentors who can guide you to success in the field of your dreams.

So child of God what is your gift?

Young people today have multiple talents and gifts that range from like singing, drawing, writing, speaking, and rapping. On the other hand many are gifted in athletics like running, football, basketball, baseball, tennis, swimming, boxing, and bowling. Sadly, many times in our circle of associates we aren't told on a practical level that we have a better chance of becoming an engineer, doctor, lawyer, accountant, professor, president, senator, CEO, or dentist, rather than a professional athlete (based on statistics) in chapter 9.

The Book of Daniel speaks of how their talents were requested in the

King's palace (1:4). We must remember that in Babylon, King Nebuchadnezzar desired to use Daniel and his friends' talents in his kingdom and how Satan desires to use our gifts today through luring us with his table of delicacies in his earthly palace. How? By prostituting their gifts and talents in strip clubs, gangs, through violence, drugs, homosexuality, pornographic music, movies and books, as well as defilement through premarital sex to name a few. The Bible says, "And whatever you do [no matter what it is] in word or in deed, do everything in the name of the Lord Jesus and in [dependence upon] His person, giving praise to God the Father through Him." (AMP, Colossians 3:17). God doesn't get glory when women and men display their naked bodies like cars on sale at a dealership. Your body is the temple of the Holy Ghost and not a recreational tool. Your body is for your spouse when you marry, not for "friends with benefits or a significant other."We glorify God with our bodies in devotion, through prayer, and on a job that doesn't disrespect God, family, self, and church. God doesn't get glory when people are addicted to the creation rather than addicted to the creator. In the Book of Genesis, God gave man dominion over the earth, not the earth dominion over man (1:28). However, we see man bowing to plants like marijuana and cocoa leaves (creation) and allowing it to determine his destiny instead of Christ Jesus our Lord. Talents and gifts are God-given and must be used to give God glory! I encourage you to keep the faith and use your skills to represent the Father in all ways.

HOW TO BE VICTORIOUS IN THE UNIVERSITY OF BABYLON

Why is the world and Satan bent on using our youth's gifts and talents?" To abort God's calling in their lives is the answer.

Jesus says:

"I am the door: by me if any man enters in, he shall be saved, and shall go in and out, and find pasture. The thief cometh not, but for to steal, and to

kill, and to destroy: I have come that they might have life, and that they might have it more abundantly."(KJV, John 10: 9-10).

How? The evidence of how King Nebuchadnezzar desired the brainwashing, re-training, and re-teaching of all his captives is found in "...and whom they might teach the learning and the tongue of the Chaldeans" (KJV, Daniel 1:4c). It is here we see a change in culture and value systems as the Hebrews assimilate into the Babylonian culture at the king's command.

From the aforementioned scripture, it is obvious that they were being enrolled in a curriculum in the University of Babylon that would influence them with the Chaldean culture. Archaeologists have uncovered thousands of clay tablets that provide with information and introduce us to Chaldean life. For example, according to John Phillips and Jerry Vines, authors of *Exploring the Book of Daniel,* "They were to be subjected to the academic, philosophical, and religious ideas of a godless civilization, to pagan philosophies and evolutionary theories. They were to be taught astronomy, in which the Chaldeans excelled and astrology, a highly developed Babylonian superstition."[1] The same wicked schemes we saw over 2,000 years ago are being implemented today in our public schools and universities, which are in direct opposition to Christ Jesus, the Bible, and teachings originating at home. I once read in Lifeway magazine that "students are leaving the church when they graduate from high school; their foundation is not strong enough to keep them in church, or at least that's true for 70% of high school graduates." Many of our young people leave home gifted and talented but not armed with the Word of God. They are faced with a hostile culture, bombarded with societal pressures, and are taught with a God-excluded secular education. How unfortunate it is that these gifts and talents lie dormant beneath a God- less culture, where the "wanna be" generation takes center stage in American way of life.

How do the parents, guardians, pastors and Sunday school teachers deal with this spiritual terrorist (Satan) and his ever changing bag of

---

1   John Phillips and Jerry Vines, *Exploring the Book of Daniel* (Neptune, New Jersey: Loizeaux Brothers, 1999), 23.

delusions? The answer is simple — the Bible. In order to protect our children and their gifts, we must first "Train up a child in the way he should go: and when he is old, he will not depart from it" (KJV, Proverbs 22:6). The Hebrew word train means "to dedicate" or "to cultivate." "This means as a caretaker — whether a parent or guardian — we must commit ourselves to godly training and discipline of our children to Christ and His will."[2] Another key work here is children. I believe much confusion can be avoided in the home if parents recognize, respect, and treat children according to their age group and maturity level.

> Remember, children are little people who do not have the ability to defend themselves against an ungodly environment, so if they can't transform, they will conform!

Provided here to help us understand and deal with the youth is a graph with a breakdown of Erik Erikson's Stages of Psychosocial Development:[3]

Infancy	Up to 1 year old
Toddler/Pre-school	1-2 years/3-5 years
Children	**6-puberty**
Adolescence	**Teen years-20's**
Young Adolescence	20s to early 40s
Middle Adulthood	40s to early 60s
Late Adulthood	Late 60's and up

This will provide us with a guideline to follow in rearing our children in the fear and admonition of the Lord.

Training children includes holiness and a separation from the world and its influences unto Christ. There are certain environments that are so toxic to our children that their talents and gifts can't be recognized. Just how destructive are certain environments to our children's talents and futures? The answers are found around us daily. Like Daniel and friends, we're living in a polytheistic nation. God tells the Prophet Ezekiel to

---

2   Donald C. Stamps, *The Full Life Study Bible* (Grand Rapids, MI: Zondervan Publishing House, 1992), 952.

3   David G. Myers, *Exploring Psychology*, 7th ed. (Holland, MI: Worth Publishers, 2008), 120.

call for a time of repentance from idols among the elders and people in Israel:

> *The word of the LORD came to me: "Son of man, if a country sins against me by being unfaithful and I stretch out my hand against it to cut off its food supply and send famine upon it and kill its people and their animals, even if these three men — Noah, Daniel and Job — were in it, they could save only themselves by their righteousness, declares the Sovereign LORD. (NIV, Ezekiel 14:12-14)*

> *"Or if I send wild beasts through that country and they leave it childless and it becomes desolate so that no one can pass through it because of the beasts, as surely as I live, declares the Sovereign LORD, even if these three men were in it, they could not save their own sons or daughters. They alone would be saved, but the land would be desolate." (NIV, Ezekiel 14:15-16)*

"Judah's moral climate had become so sinful that the righteous prayers of Noah, Daniel, and Job would not be sufficient to save even their own children. Believers must be very careful about the social and educational environment in which they place their children. It may become so ungodly that neither our righteous living nor our fervent prayers will be enough to bring them to accept Christ as their Lord and Savior."[4]

In light of what was just mentioned, Noah, Daniel, and Jobs' character, identity, and personality have already been established in God at this point in time. Due primarily to their age and relationship with God they were spiritually covered and protected. Unfortunately, the children, teens, and young adults who fail to see committed living to Christ generally mimic this behavior and fail to commit to a dedicated relationship with Jesus making for spiritual vulnerability to attack.

We as parents/guardians must encourage and influence our children to pursue God for themselves. The Apostle Paul put it best, "Wherefore I put thee into remembrance that you stir up the gift of God, which is in thee by the putting on of my hands. For God hath not given us

---

4 Donald C. Stamps, *The Full Life Study Bible* (Grand Rapids, MI: Zondervan Publishing House, 1992), 1193-1194.

the spirit of fear, but of power, and of love, and of a sound mind." (2 Timothy 1:6-7). *Charisma* (Χάρισμα) in the Greek means gift. This was given to Paul's young protégé Timothy which is compared to a fire that he must "stir or fan into flames" in accordance to the scripture. "This gift was probably a special gift that takes the power from the Holy Spirit to fulfill his ministry."[5] The power of God and this ministry gift doesn't only flow through the Pastor, but through the young people as well. We are ambassadors from heaven representing the Kingdom of God and the ministry gift of charisma is empowerment for service unto Christ. These gifts however don't automatically stay strong; Paul had to tell Timothy to "stir up" the gift of God. This is done by praying, praising God, obedience, faithfulness, and loving Him. The only way some people will see or get acquainted with Christ is through His children using their "charisma." For example, when the world sees a true believer as a teacher, they see Christ as a teacher; when the world sees a true believer as a gospel artist, they see Christ as a gospel artist. Jesus states, "Let your light so shine before men, that they may see your good works, and glorify your father which is in heaven" (KJV, Matthew 5:16).

The Apostle Paul also teaches about fear. He says, "For God hath not given us the spirit of fear, but of power, and of love, and of a sound mind." We don't have to walk in fear — false evidence appearing real — when we can walk in faith. Child of God, Christ has given us the power to walk upright, the love to act right, and a sound mind to live right! Don't allow fear to choke the charisma in your life.

As we return to Proverbs 22:6b — "and when he is old, he will not depart from it" — we see that children who are trained in the ways of God, Word of God, fear of God, admonition of God, and have a true relationship with Christ will not depart from the teachings of their parents. Though this is true, we live in a fallen world and many reject Christ and are unfaithful to His Word. Children, for example, can be unfaithful to God and influenced to sin and given into temptation as well. The Book of James sheds light on this point:

---

5   Donald C. Stamps, *The Full Life Study Bible* (Grand Rapids, MI: Zondervan Publishing House, 1992), 1918.

"Let no man say when he is tempted, I am tempted of God: for God cannot be tempted with evil, neither tempteth he any man: But every man is tempted when he is drawn away of his own lust, and enticed. Then when lust hath conceived, it bringeth forth sin: and sin, when it finished, bringeth forth death. Do not err, my beloved brethren. Every good gift and every perfect gift is from above, and cometh down from the Father of Lights, with whom is no variableness, neither shadow of turning." (KJV, 1:13-17).

With this being said, regardless of your mistakes and failures get up, shake off the past in Jesus' name and confess these things to Christ. Live for Him because you are a gift from heaven regardless of the color, shape, size, damage of the gift, and past mistakes. God can redeem the time and recreate who you are.

EXPECT SUCCESS

Now that we have established a foundation for identifying talents and gifts, protecting your gifts, and walking in faith, we can now expect success. God's ways are unlike our ways. Society measures success based on financial status, amounts of boyfriends/girlfriends you have, social status, and material possessions; God measures success by the relationship man has with Him. Bishop Jordan sums up the topic of success with his words:

"People who are successful know, with the same certainty that you know the sun will rise in the morning, that if they make the leap of faith, no matter what happens they will somehow land okay and make the best of whatever occurs.

And let me tell you, God shows great favor to those who do that!"[6]

"We must expect greatness from ourselves. You cannot succeed with an attitude of weakness, doubt, and fear. Conquer with your eye first, then conquer with your hand. Faith annihilates obstacles and moves mountains. Abraham, Joshua, Moses, and

---

6   E. Bernard Jordan, The Laws of Thinking (USA: Hay House, Inc, 2006), 231.

others were able to perform miracles through faith. Without it you can do nothing. A strong man loses power when he loses confidence in his ability to act in faith. You must train yourself to have no doubt in your ability to create the best outcomes — You must always act like a winner and emit winning ideas!"[7]

God desires success for His people in every area of life. Success isn't possible without putting into practice the measure of faith that He has already given you. As you take steps of faith, you will begin to see your dreams and what you have worked hard for become apparent.

DISCUSSION QUESTIONS

1. What were Daniel and his friends' talents and gifts?
2. What is your talent of gift?
3. What is the Greek word for gift?
4. What are the prerequisites for "stirring up" your gifts?
5. Explain Proverbs 22:6.
6. What is the difference between adolescents and young adults?
7. Should parents/guardians rear children the same way as adolescents?
8. How does God measure success?
9. How does the world and society measure success?

---

7   Ibid., 231.

NOTES

CHAPTER 4

THE 10 DAY TEENAGE FAST/DIET

"The King assigned them a daily amount of food and wine from the King's table. They were to be trained for three years, and after that they were to enter the King's service" (NIV, Daniel 1:5)

"But Daniel resolved not to defile himself with the royal food and wine, and he asked the chief official for permission not to defile himself this way. Now God had caused the official to show favor and sympathy to Daniel, but the official told Daniel, 'I am afraid of my lord the king, who has assigned your food and drink. Why should he see you looking worse than the other young men your age? The king would then have my head because of you.' Daniel then said to the guard whom the chief official had appointed over Daniel, Hananiah, Mishael and Azariah, Please test your servants for ten days: Give us nothing but vegetables to eat and water to drink" (NIV, Daniel 1:8-12)

GOING AGAINST THE GRAIN

Remember the old adage, "We are what we eat"? Over 2,000 years ago, Daniel and his friends were well-aware of this concept. God gave them favor to go against the culture of eating food prepared by King Nebuchadnezzar of Babylon. Carl F. Keil and F. Delitzsch, authors of *Commentary of the Old Testament,* mention that "The partaking of food brought to them from the king's table was contaminating, not so much because the food was not prepared according to the Levitical ordinance — or not because it consisted of the flesh of animals which to the Israelites were unclean — but the reason of their rejection of it was, that the heathen at their feast offered up in sacrifice to their gods, a part of the food and the drink, and thus consecrated their meals by a religious right; whereby not only he who participated in such a meal participated in the worship of idols, but the meat and the wine as a whole were the meat and the wine of an idol sacrifice, partaking of which, according to the saying of the apostle (1 Cor. 10:20f.), is the same as sacrificing to devils." The Bible forbids eating any food sacrificed to gods, the worship of idols and false gods even in this twenty-first century. Covetousness and unclean cravings to place something before God and take His place is sin. For example, when one idolizes athletes, entertainers, or public figures and desires to be like them and please them at all costs can be a sign of compromise. This was something Daniel and friends weren't willing to do.

TEENAGE FASTING AND DIET

Daniel, in order not to defile himself and his comrades, had twice requested a ten day fast as written in the Scriptures: "Please test your servants for ten days, and let us be given some vegetables to eat and water to drink." (NAS, Daniel 1:12) This Scripture passage reveals that the purpose of fasting is to seek and to know God. Fasting can be defined as abstaining from eating food, but not water and prayer. There are several fasts in the Bible:

Prayer & Fasting

- Daniel's fast consisted of foods such as vegetables, fruits, nuts, and water — also known as a partial fast (Daniel 1:10-12).
- Jesus' fast was for forty days in the wilderness. After it was completed, He became hungry (not thirsty). He refrained from food but not water (Luke 4:1-2).

In the Book of Isaiah, God reveals to believers His purpose and reason for fasting:

"Is such a fast as yours what I have chosen, a day for a man to humble himself with sorrow in his soul? [Is true fasting merely mechanical?] Is it only to bow down his head like a bulrush and to spread sackcloth and ashes under him [to indicate a condition of heart that he does not have?] Will you call this a fast and an acceptable day to the Lord? [Rather] is not this the fast that I have chosen: to loose the bonds of wickedness, to undo the bands of the yoke, to let the oppressed go free, and that you break every [enslaving] yoke (AMP, 58:5-6)?

There are also spiritual and practical benefits to fasting. Prayer and fasting curb the appetite for sex, drugs, and other nasty habits. Also, they help people deal with, emotional struggles, improve medical conditions, draw people to a closer relationship with God, help believers sense the leading of the Lord, and even improve a person's physical appearance. The mind is sharpened and the spirit is strengthened, which helps believers to endure and to withstand the pressures of the world. It is advisable to consult your pastor, physician, and/or parent(s) for guidance on where to start and how to go about fasting and praying.

THE DANIEL DIET /FAST

> **COOL FACTS**
>
> *Daniel prayed 3x's a day toward Jerusalem (Dan. 6:10-11).*

The Daniel diet was based on the Biblical principles of dieting "passed down through the generations since Adam, according to Daniel 1:10-12, the diet chosen by Daniel consisted of vegetables and water. Nearly all Bible translators interpret this diet using the words vegetables, pulse or even grain. The authors of the King James Version of the Bible chose the word pulse. The word pulse is used in some translations because pulse is actual seeds like legumes and those seeds from pods." As we looked at many biblical examples like Moses, Elijah, Daniel, Esther, Paul and Christ, prayer along with fasting/dieting led to some sort of divine intervention from God.

BIBLE DIET FOODS

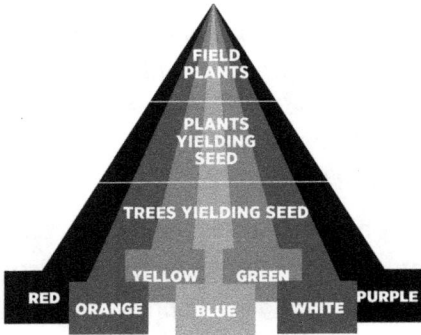

Four Bible Food Groups

1. **Trees** whose edible yield is bearing seed or is seeds.

2. **Plants** whose edible yield is bearing seed or is seeds.

3. **Field plants** which are herbs, roots, and leafy vegetables.

4. **Clean Meat**[1] according to biblical standards

Rainbow Foods Bible dieting is simple! The foods are color coded.

RAINBOW FOODS

Our food was created to be appealing to all of our senses – especially taste, smell, and sight. Within the skin pigments and edible portion of these living foods, there lies a vast array of phytonutrients. Most of these have yet to be fully understood or documented by science. Be joyful and eat for an abundant life.[2]

RED FOODS:
Trees: cherries, apples, cranberries, papaya, pomegranate
Plants: tomatoes, strawberries, watermelon, raspberries
Herbs: beets, rhubarb, radishes
Nutrient: Lycopene

ORANGE FOODS:
Trees: oranges, grapefruit, peaches
Plants: pumpkin, squash

---

1   Ibid

2   Ibid

Herbs: carrots, sweet potatoes, yams
Nutrient: beta-carotene

YELLOW FOODS:

Trees: lemons, pears, apricots, grapefruit

Plants: corn, squash, wheat, cantaloupe

Herbs: rutabagas

Nutrient: vitamin C

GREEN FOODS:

Trees: avocados, olives, pears, lime

Plants: cucumbers, peas, green beans, zucchini

Herbs: broccoli, asparagus, greens, spinach, brussels sprouts, kale, celery, green onions

Nutrient: lutein

BLUE FOODS:

Plants: blueberries, blackberries, mulberries

Nutrient: Anthocyanins

WHITE FOODS:

Trees: coconut, dates, pears, nuts

Plants: white beans, oats

Herbs: onions, cauliflower, garlic, horseradish, potatoes, turnips, mushrooms, parsnips, shallots, ginger

Nutrient: Allicin

PURPLE FOODS:

Trees: plums, prunes, figs

Plants: grapes, blackberries, elderberries

Herbs: beets, eggplants, cabbage[3] There is no mention of nutrients or purple foods from this site.

The truth is, people need more fruits and vegetables in their diets in

---

3   Ibid.

order to compete mentally, be emotionally stable, and be physically healthy. Let's get practical, the number seven is used many times throughout the bible as God's number for perfection. For example:

Seven is the biblical number for perfection

- For example, on the 7th day God rested from all His work.
- God told Noah to take 7 of every kind of clean animal, male and female, into the ark. (NIV, Genesis 7:2)
- God told Joshua, "Have 7 priests carry trumpets of rams horns in front of the ark. On the 7th day march around the city 7 times, with priest blowing the trumpets." (NIV, Joshua 6:4)
- There are 7 colors in the rainbow which represents God's covenant with Noah, all of mankind, and serves as a reminder to Israel that He will never destroy the Earth by water (flood) again.

There are many benefits from eating from the 7 rainbow colors:

RED FOODS

"Apples prevent constipation, control diabetes, prevent cancer, and lower the risk of heart disease. The healing power is in the skin! Fiber, fiber, fiber. 'An apple a day, keeps the doctor away.'

Strawberries are also known for vitamin C which boosts the immune system and fights colds."

ORANGE FOODS

"Grapefruits are known for their citrus taste. They are known to prevent cancer, reduce bruising, relieve cold symptoms, and prevent heart disease and strokes.

Pumpkins, also known for beta-carotene, improve night vision, boost the immune system, and prevent macular degeneration, heart disease, and cancer.

For you sweet potato fans out there, your favored veggie is packed with antioxidants. Sweet potatoes healing power is in its ability to preserve memory, to control diabetes, and to reduce the risk of heart disease and cancer."

YELLOW FOODS

"Apricots contain beta-carotene. This important nutrient converts into vitamin A which both protects the eyes and acts as a powerful antioxidant used to fight free radicals.

Cantaloupe is known as the fruit of circulation. It helps to lower high blood pressure and cholesterol, prevents cataracts, and reduces the risk of both heart disease and cancer. Also, this fruit is rich in both vitamin C and beta-carotene."

GREEN FOODS

"Avocados are known to prevent birth defects, control cholesterol, and lower blood pressure. They are, also, used as a beauty agent on the faces of many women.

Peas help prevent cancer and heart disease as well as relieve cold symptoms.

Broccoli protects against heart disease, fights off cancer, and boosts immunity."

BLUE FOODS

"Amazingly, blueberries and blackberries are great in preventing hemorrhoids"

WHITE FOODS

"Pears are a renowned cholesterol fighting fruit. Its skin contains fiber which prevents constipation and, hemorrhoids as well as reduces the risk colon cancer

Oats are known to absorb cholesterol like a sponge, to improve insulin sensitivity and to reduce the risk of heart disease and cancer.

Onions, although difficult to peal without tearing up, can lower blood pressure, reduce inflammation, and decrease the risk of cancer."

PURPLE FOODS

"Figs were Cleopatra's favorite fruit. They are known to lower high blood pressure, prevent colon cancer, relieve constipation, and control cholesterol.

Beets, of which I'm not a fan, are known for preventing birth defects and protecting against cancer."[4]

BIBLE FOODS AND THE PYRAMID

There are two pyramids that I want to discuss in this section. One pyramid is the Mediterranean Diet introduced in 1993 by Harvard School of Public Health and the European Office of World Health Organization and the other pyramid the USDA Food Guide and FDA Recommended daily allowances.

The Mediterranean diet consists of regular physical exercise daily, fruits, vegetables, nuts, breads, grain, seeds, fish, seafood, poultry, eggs, cheese, meats and sweets. The author by no means endorses the casual drinking of wine with or without food only for medicinal reasons. According to a CNN health report on March 11, 2007 "Mediterranean diet cuts heart, diabetes risk factors." Furthermore many of the basic food groups in the Mediterranean Diet in order of importance are in the Bible.

The USDA released a newly revised pyramid called MyPyramid. The design of this pyramid includes colored stripped bands of various widths to represent the food groups and portions sizes Americans ought to eat. It also includes grains, vegetables, fruit, dairy, and meats and beans. Included at the base of these diets are exercises for health reasons. A question asks many times in bible study did Jesus exercise during His time on the earth? Well, during Christ thirty-three years on this earth, He didn't have the convenience of cars, SUVs, or public transportation, so he walked or rode a donkey to Jerusalem for Passover, Pentecost, and Feast of weeks or just ordinary travel during the early years of the first century. (KJV, Matthew 21:1-21, John 7:1) As one can see there was a lot of exercising/walking in the bible for example from Bethlehem to Jerusalem is about five miles, or from Nazareth to Jerusalem about 70 miles.

---

4   Selene Yeager, *The Doctors Book of Food Remedies,* ed. (United States: Rodale, Inc., 1998).

CHAPTER 4

HERBS OF THE FIELD

He causes the grass to grow for the cattle, and herb for the
service of man: that he may bring forth food out of the earth.
(KJV, Psalms 104:14)

Just as God made the grass for the cow to eat to meet its nutritional
needs, He also made herbs in the fields to meet our nutritional needs
for both taste and medicinal purposes. For example, it is a scientific fact
that the healing power of herbs can help "prevent infections, ease pain
and swelling, relieve menopausal and lower cholesterol."[5] It's obvious to
see God takes care of His creation by providing the necessary elements
to keep it going.

EATING MEAT IN THE NEW TESTAMENT

The Bible says that when Peter went to the house top to pray, in the
sixth hour he became hungry and fell into a trance. He describes this
trance in great detail in the Book of Acts. Peter says,

> *And he saw Heaven opened and a certain vessel descending*
> *unto him, as it had been a great sheet knit at the four corners,*
> *and let down to the earth. Wherein were all manner of four*
> *footed beasts of the earth, and wild beasts, and creeping things,*
> *and fowls of the air. And there came a voice to him, Rise, Peter;*
> *kill, and eat. But Peter said, not so, Lord; for I have never eaten*
> *anything that is common or unclean. And the voice spake unto*
> *him again the second time, what God hath cleanse, that call not*
> *thou common (KJV, Acts 10: 11-16).*

This is a topic my students ask questions about all the time. Questions
like can we eat pork? So let's investigate what the bible says about
eating meat in the New Testament. In Peter's vision in Acts 10:11, he
witnessed a large sheet with four corners coming down out of heaven
upon the earth — this reminds me of a father who spreads a linen cloth
on the ground at the beach before he barbeques. In verse 12 inside

---

5   Ibid.

> **COOL FACT**
>
> *Katharizo is a Greek verb for clean meaning to ceremonially, spiritually, and literally cleanse!*

the large sheet were all kinds of four-footed animals and crawling creatures of the earth, and the birds of the sky. Also, we see in Genesis 1:26 some examples of these types of animals like "cattle, birds and the creeping things like land animals. Next in verse 13 Peter heard a voice say "Rise, Peter; kill, and eat." In verse 14 Peter answered the Lord saying "No so, Lord; for I have never eaten anything common or unclean." Peter viewed four-footed animals and crawling creatures (like pork or beef) as unclean by Jewish standards, because he refused to eat them in verse 13. The Lord spoke to him a second time, "Do not call anything impure that God has made clean." It's okay to eat culturally diverse food in moderation (KJV, Philippians 4:5).

In the Book of Mark, Jesus rebukes the Pharisees (religious people) for their hypocritical views of his disciples when they failed to wash their hands before they ate (Chapter 7). Jesus goes on to explain what defiles a man. In other words, He clarifies what renders a person to be unclean. Is it the food (meat, pork, etc.) that goes into the body? Or, is it what comes out of the heart? Let's listen to Jesus, "There is nothing from without a man, that entering into him can defile him: but the things which come out of him, those are they that defile the man" (KJV, Mark 7:15). A practical illustration on this matter would be how religious people are concerned about how dirty the outside of a cup is, rather than how dirty the inside of a cup is before drinking out of it. This metaphor is a reflection of the Pharisees and how they scrutinize the lives of people. This is hypocrisy at its best! The Apostle Paul states, "Therefore let no one sit in judgment on you in matters of food and drink, or with regard to a feast day or a New Moon or a Sabbath.

> **COOL FACT**
>
> *The basic Old Testament requirements, as defined in Leviticus 11 and Deuteronomy 14, for eating clean and unclean meat were for Israel when they were under the Mosaic Covenant.*

Such [things] are only the shadow of things that are to come, and they have only a symbolic value. But the reality (the substance, the solid fact of what is foreshadowed, the body of it) belongs to Christ." (AMP, Colossians 2:16-17). The Bible makes it clear that food does not spiritually contaminate a man's spirit. On the other hand, what comes out of his heart, can destroy him.

Daniel and friends were not eating fast food or junk food. Instead, they healthy food — fruits and vegetables that God created to nurture the body. In closing, fruits and vegetables are beneficial for the human body (Daniel's diet proved this!) Daniel's overcoming was a result of his faith and was proof that he served the real King. According to scripture, Daniel faced tests and trials but conquered them all through prayer, fasting, and God's Word. He wasn't bashful to approach God and this is what gave him victory! The result of this ten day fast was apparent, the King found them ten times better than all the magicians and astrologers that were in his entire realm. This outcome will be elaborated on in the last chapter.

TEEN OBESITY IN AMERICA

Statistics show that teen obesity has grown to epidemic portions in the U.S. This article will review teen obesity statistics, take a look at what causes teen obesity, and suggest activities to help reduce teen obesity.

Today America is facing one of its greatest challenges with our youth, one of many being teenage obesity. Obesity is defined as being disproportionately overweight for a specific height. America's future doctors, lawyers, engineers, teachers, servicemen/women accountants, and others are overweight and are in poor health. This is a new phenomenon in this country that has never been seen before. According to the Center for Disease Control and Prevention (CDC) statistics, "Childhood obesity has more than tripled in the past 30 years. The percentage of adolescents 12-19 years in

> **COOL FACT**
>
> Food sacrificed to idols or gods are forbidden (1 Corinthians 8:1-13).

the United States who were obese increased from 5% in 1980 to nearly 18% in 2008."[6] The present effects of teenage obesity are physical, mental, emotional and social health problems. The present physical health problems for these overweight teenagers are possibly pre-diabetic symptoms or cardiovascular disease. The mental/emotional affects range from low self-esteem, depression, struggle with various issues and even difficulties talking about these challenges. The social result of obesity can be from not getting along with peers to promiscuity for acceptance.

WHAT CAUSES TEEN OBESITY?

Teen obesity is becoming an epidemic in America and around the world. The main causes of teenage obesity are poor eating habits and lack of exercise. When I was a teenager we exercised before, during, and after school and even on weekends. For example, we walked to school, participated in a physical education class for at least an hour, and walked home from school. On the weekends chores were completed in the morning, so you could play football, basketball or baseball all day, except Sundays. As you already know, God rested on the seventh day, and so did we by attending church. Television was watched at night after school, once chores were completed in the living room. Today, teenagers are watching television in their rooms unsupervised, as well as browsing the internet due to the explosion of social media with little or no exercise. "The factors that contribute to morbid obesity amongst teens are cultural influences, genetics, and personal behaviors, according to the American Academy of Child and Adolescent Psychiatry. If one of the parents is obese then the teenager has a 50% chance to become obese...."[7] So parents we have our work cut out for us, the fight against teenage obesity starts with us, we must prepare, cook and eat healthy foods; likewise teens will follow us. Also, our young people need to eat less junk food, have yearly checkups, daily exercise and eat the seven colors of God's rainbow every day.

---

6   http://www.cdc.gov/healthyyouth/obesity/facts.htm

7   http://www.obesity.ygoy.com/obesity-teens/

For most people, their diets too often consist of greasy fast food, sugary snacks, and large, restaurant-sized portions. <u>Going on a strict diet is not necessarily the answer.</u> It is important to change the way the *whole* family eats. Whole fruits, whole vegetables, and whole grains should make up a large part of a person's daily diet. For instance, parents need to know the value of choosing whole grain breads rather than white ones. The August 2002 issue of *The American Journal of Clinical Nutrition* contains a report showing that "When you eat foods made with flour, your blood sugar rises quickly. Whole grains are like capsules that release their contents very slowly. It takes about an hour to cook whole grains because of this tight capsule, and your body still has a difficult time breaking the capsule, so they are very slow to digest. Whole grains help prevent diabetes and obesity because they keep insulin levels lower."[8] This outcome was true no matter how much refined grain and fiber were eaten.

Recent reports from public health organizations have concluded that when children are given appealing places to play, it increases their participation. As a result, their health was markedly improved and teen obesity was reduced.

ACTIVITIES TO DO TO HELP TEENS STAY FIT:

- Take walks
- Play basketball
- Play tennis
- Play volleyball
- Play racquetball
- Go to a skate park
- Go swimming
- Play any ball sports

---

8   American Journal of Clinical Nutrition, Vol. 76, No. 2, 390-398, August 2002. Whole-grain intake is favorably associated with metabolic risk factors for type 2 diabetes and cardiovascular disease in the Framingham Offspring Study1,2,3,4 Nicola , McKeown, James B Meigs, Simin Liu, Peter WF Wilson and Paul F Jacques.

These activities can all make a big difference in teen obesity. Additionally, there are classes in dance, gymnastics, karate, and other types of exercise. There are youth baseball, football and soccer teams to join. The idea is to choose something fun to get moving, dancing, jumping, climbing, walking, or skating. So, grab an apple, and go have fun![9]

COOL FACT

Dr. John Ratey says "Exercise doesn't make you smarter, but it optimizes the brain for learning."[10]

More studies have concluded that exercise and physical activity increases positive brain performance. Dr. John Ratey, an associate professor of psychiatry at Harvard Medical School, wrote in his book *Spark: The Revolutionary New Science of Exercise and the Brain*[11] that even regular brisk walks can boost memory, alleviate stress, enhance intelligence, and allay aggression. In closing, God abolished the dietary laws of the Mosaic Law. As Christians, you are still responsible for being good stewards of your bodies, which means you are required to eat healthy. It is clear that your bodies are the temple of the Holy Spirit. It is also apparent that people need regular exercise, good diet, and a healthy lifestyle to maintain wellness and to remain available to be used by God.

DISCUSSION QUESTIONS

1. If we are all God's people, why did He designate different diets to the Israelites?

2. Speaking of the rainbow, what does it represent related to good health?

3. Do believers really need to fast?

    a. What is the purpose of fasting?

    b. Can I do without fasting?

---

9   "Trouble Teen 101" http://www.troubledteen101.com. Copyright @ 2009 Trouble Teen 101-Help for Troubled Teen Issues.

10   John Ratey and Eric Hagerman, *Spark: The Revolutionary New Science of Exercise and the Brain*, (New York: Hatchet Book Group) 2008.

11   Ibid.

c.   What are the effects of fasting?

4.   What are the benefits of fruits and vegetables?

5.   Can believers eat meat including pork?

6.   Name one of the "Red Foods" and its God-given benefits.

7.   Name one of the "Green Foods" and its God-given benefits.

8.   What was Cleopatra's favorite fruit? What is its benefit?

9.   What two Bible foods did Daniel's ten day fast consist of?

10. What are some of the causes of teen obesity? Name two solutions.

NOTES

CHAPTER 5

THE ATTEMPT TO CHANGE IDENTITIES

"Among these were some from Judah: Daniel, Hananiah,
Mishael, and Azariah. The chief official gave them new names:
to Daniel, the name Belteshazzar; to Hananiah, Shadrach; to
Mishael, Meshach; and to Azariah, Abednego"
(NIV, Daniel 1:6-7).

WHAT'S IN A NAME?

Names are what make every person unique and is what we all inevitably answer to; and the adoption of a nick-name or the changing of a name can alter self-image and even self-esteem. At this point in time in scripture Daniel and friends find themselves in a critical spiritual situation because their names are being changed. King Nebuchadnezzar's evil plan was to remove from these young men of Judah any trace of adoration for the Lord and to keep before them the worship of the Chaldean's gods. Nebuchadnezzar was not comfortable allowing these young boys names to be a constant reminder of their faith in the Lord, so he changes them to try to create a spiritual identity crisis. How? The significance of their godly names illuminates how their newly imposed names are a device to aid in the destruction of the name of Israel's true God. All four names of Daniel and friends honor Israel's God, Yahweh. "Yah is an abbreviation for Yahweh or Jehovah."[1] In the Old Testament, Yahweh was honored when children were named at birth after Him. According to *The Old Testament Bible Knowledge Commentary,* the name "Daniel" means "God is my judge" which is changed to "Belteshazzar" which means "Lady, protect the king." In addition, "Hananiah" means"Yahweh has been gracious"which is changed to "Shadrach" meaning "I am

---

1   Phillips, and Jerry Vines. *Exploring the Book of Daniel.* Neptune, New Jersey: Loizeaux Brothers, 1999, PG. 25

fearful (of a god)." Mishael's name means "who is what God is" which is changed to Meshach, meaning "I am despised, contemptible, humbled (before my god)." Finally, "Azariah" means "Yahweh has helped" which is changed to "Abednego" which means "servant of Nebo" in Chaldean mythology, Nebo is the son of Bel, and he was the Babylonian god of writing and vegetation.[2]

I can imagine that there were many more young people than just four; however, the Bible only mentions Daniel and his friends. I believe as the other young children of Israel were absorbed into the Babylonian culture, they conformed to the will of King Nebuchadnezzar instead of being transformed daily by the renewing of their minds with the Word of God. Scripture warns against this type of behavior, "And be not conformed to this world: but be ye transformed by the renewing of your mind, that ye may prove what is that good, and acceptable, and perfect, will of God" (KJV, Romans 12:2).

Just as Daniel and friends were transformed daily through the Word of God, you too can stand against things of the world and be transformed. Christian believers must remember that "transformation" in the Greek is [μεταμορφοω] "metamorphoo"; this Greek verb is in the present imperative tense rendering a command in the present. It is where we get the word metamorphosis to change into another form. The idea of a caterpillar changing into a butterfly comes to mind. The bible commands us not to be a carbon copy of the world, but of Jesus Christ. For example, God changed Moses from a murderer to a deliverer, David from a shepherd boy into a king, Gideon from a coward to a warrior, Peter from unstable Simon to Peter (stone) and Saul was transformed (changed) into another man. (1 Samuel 10:6-9). Today allow the Holy Spirit to indwell, comfort, seal, teach, lead, empower, sanctify and change you into a disciple of the lord Jesus Christ.

---

2   John F. Walvoord and Roy B. Zuck, *The Bible Knowledge Commentary on the Old Testament* (Grand Rapids, MI: Zondervan Publishers, 1985), 1130.

WHAT'S YOUR NAME?

We live in a culture that names are used to define and identify business, entertainers, colleges, countries, music, and sports positive or negative. But how far are people or families willing to go to express themselves through names. "You can tell a lot about a society by the kind of names it gives to its children. There was a time in this country when parents named children after Bible characters. Now they are named after rock musicians, movie stars,"[3] hip hop rappers, Greek gods, fictional characters and expensive cars. Bishop E. Bernard Jordan, author of The Laws of Thinking, speaks about names and the nature of it so eloquently:

> *How you name things reveals much about how you regard the world. If you are aware of the power of naming, then you will exercise care in what you name the things and people in your life — and how you name yourself. For the name of a thing not only reveals its true nature, it sets the definition of its nature in motion. In naming something or someone, you alter its nature.*[4]

NAMES AND PERSONALITIES

How do these names take on personalities? "The term personality derives from the Latin word persona, which refers to a mask used by actors in a play. It is easy to see how persona came to refer to outward appearance, the public face we display around us. Based on its deprivation, then, we might conclude that personality refers to our eternal invisible characteristics, those aspects of us that other people can see. Our personality would then be defined in terms of the impression we make on others — that is, what we appear to be."[5]

The standard dictionary defines "personality" as the as the internal and external aspects of one's character that influence behavior in

---

3   John Phillips and Jerry Vines, *Exploring the Book of Daniel* (Neptune, New Jersey: Loizeaux Brothers, 1999), 23.

4   E. Bernard Jordan, *The Laws of Thinking* (USA: Hay House, Inc, 2006), 119-120.

5   Daune P. Schultz and Sydney Ellen Schultz, *Theories of Personality*, 9th ed. (Belmont, CA: Wadsworth, Cengage Learning, 2009), 8-9.

different situations. The world pulls at teenagers and young adults like a puppet-master with strings. If they surrender to the world, they begin to act out what they hear through their ear-gate, see through their eye-gate and speak through their mouth-gate. King Solomon provides a well-known proverb that deals with the mind and heart of men, "For as he thinks in his heart, so is he" (AMP, Proverbs 23:7a). So, when a man thinks he is a gangster because of his "street-name," generally, his world view changes. As a self-fulfilling prophecy, he lives and dies as a gangster (although this may not be who he is). When teenagers embrace negative stereotypes, they mask their personalities (as defined earlier) as an impersonator and they mimic the very thing(s) that will eventually destroy them. How do changes in names, kinds of names, and meanings of names affect young people's identity today? Erik Erikson, known psychologist, provides a working definition of self-image with the term *ego identity.* Ego identity is defined as "the self-image formed during adolescence that integrates our ideas of what we are and what we want to be."[6] It's a known fact that between the ages of 12-18 adolescents discover their identities; on the other hand, this age group is strategically assaulted by the post-modern culture in hopes of creating an identity crisis so that they will reject the absolute truth about God and not tap into who they really are in Him. Despite this sad statement, this developmental period is when many people make a choice to follow God and develop an identity centered on Him.

Identity crisis is defined as "the failure to achieve ego identity during adolescence."[7] How? According to Erik Erickson, "those who fail to achieve a cohesive identity — who experience identity crises — will exhibit a confusion of roles. They don't seem to know who or what they are, where they belong, or where they want to go. They may withdraw from

COOL FACT

The new names given to Daniel and friends were titles of Babylon's gods & idols.

---

6   Daune P. Schultz and Sydney Ellen Schultz, *Theories of Personality*, 9th ed. (Belmont, CA: Wadsworth, Cengage Learning, 2009), 215.

7   Ibid. 216.

normal life sequence (education, job, and marriage) as Erickson did for a time or seek a negative identity in crime or drugs. Even a negative identity, as society defines it, is preferable to no identity, although it is not a satisfactory as a positive identity. Erickson noted the potentially strong impact of peer groups on the development of ego identity in adolescence. He noted that excessive association with fanatical groups and cults or obsessive identification with icons or popular culture could restrict a developing ego."[8]

I believe that the plan of Satan (like King Nebuchadnezzar) is to create an identity crisis among our young people today by changing their names through the culture and even through tradition. Some examples of nicknames are "big dog," "chino," "pimp," "killa," "little mama," "dime piece," "juicy," and "gangsta." These names have the ability to take on personalities which young people often act out. How? For instance, the name "killa" is associated with murder, violence, and crime. By putting these names, labels, nicknames, and aka's on young people, they (the name) have the potential to erase any memory of our Lord and Savior Jesus Christ in their lives. As a result of taking on false personalities, many will abort their relationship with Christ, and even stop going to church to make fast money. How? A large percentage of people drop-out of high school, church, college, or technical school in order to fulfill self-destructive lifestyles as "thugs" or "gangsters." This inevitably results in police arrests. The good news in this situation is that teens have the ability to not fall prey to the adoption of evil thoughts, names, and deeds.

CHOOSE YOU THIS DAY WHO WILL YOU SERVE, CHRIST OR MAMMON (MONEY)

Many young people ask, "What's wrong with the desire to be rich?" Provided here is one of the most shocking announcements made by Christ; He says: "How hardly shall they that have riches enter into the kingdom of God! For it is easier for a camel to go through a needle's eye,

---

8 Ibid.

than for a rich man to enter into the kingdom of God" (KJV, Luke 18:24b-25). Why? The Bible equates the hunt for wealth and covetousness with idolatry. For example, when people are willing to steal, to murder, to destroy, to manipulate, to intimidate, to dominate, they are bewitched by Satan. He is like a puppet master pulling their strings and dangling money in front of them. In the Book of Matthew, Jesus says "No man can serve two masters: for either he will hate the one, and love the other; or else he will hold to the one, and despise the other. Ye cannot serve God and mammon." (KJV, 6:24). The pursuit of possessions and a craving to be rich causes enslavement. Instead having dominion over possessions in Christ, possessions have dominion over them. For many people, riches are a barrier to salvation. Jesus says, "He also that received seed among the thorns is he that heareth the word; and the care of this world, and the deceitfulness of riches, choke the word, and he becometh unfruitful" (KJV, Matthew 13:22). This scripture is similar to a common practice in churches today. People attend church services and listen to the message, but their minds are absent. They are focused on money, houses, contracts, plans, jobs, store sales, and clothes. It is unfortunate that they are missing out on a potentially life changing message in favor of finite or temporary things that cannot save their souls.

MONEY WILL BUY...

- a bed not sleep
- books not brains
- food not appetite
- finery not beauty
- house not a home
- medicine not health
- luxuries not culture
- amusements not happiness
- a crucifix not a savior
- religion not salvation
- a good life not eternal life
- a passport not Heaven[9]

The media offers a one-sided view of the rich and famous; it flaunts their possessions, wealth, and prestige but neglects to tell the entire truth. The prime examples are in Hollywood where the professional athletes and entertainers are rich and famous, yet they are committing suicide, and

---

9   Robert J. Morgan, *Nelson's Complete Book of Short Stories, Illustrations, and Quotes* (Nashville, TN: Thomas Nelson Publishers, 2000), 575.

abusing drugs. We lived in a world full of choices, some are whether to attend a university or college, others are whether to register for the SAT or ACT, others are whether to participate in a sport this year. Everything in life boils down to a choice. For example, when someone chose to commit a crime that's a choice they made, and the dire consequences that comes along with it. The Bible admonishes believers to live a different way, "And if it seem evil unto you to serve the LORD, choose you this day whom ye will serve; whether the gods which your fathers served that were on the other side of the flood, or the gods of the Amorites, in whose land ye dwell: but as for me and my house, we will serve the LORD" (KJV, Joshua 24:15). Everyone sooner or later must make an eternal choice, whether to serve the Lord or not, why not make a choice today and choose life in Jesus Christ.

God is not against you having things; He is against things having you. He is against the pursuit of riches at all costs, and He is against riches without Him. God chose Abram and vowed to bless him and make his name great (Genesis 12:1-3). The next chapter reveals that, Abram became "very rich in cattle, in silver, and in gold" (KJV, Genesis 13:2). The difference here is that God made him rich and that Abram did not pursue riches. Instead, he pursued God. In the Book of Genesis, God declares He will "make your name great," and He did just that (KJV, Genesis 12:2c) Abraham could not make his own name great. Just like you or your abilities cannot make your name great, neither can the media, producers, fans, or family do likewise. An Christ can, though, if it is in God's will! The greatness I am referring to is a temporary and conditional greatness that comes from the world; however, the greatness that is bestowed upon Abraham is unconditional and continuous because God made a promise to him due to his faith. Jesus states, "But he that is greatest among you shall be your servant" (KJV, Matt. 23:11). In this verse Christ is giving the formula for success in the kingdom of God, one must be a servant first, and then Christ will exalt you in due season, which contradicts what the world considers great. Next verse He gives the specifics on being a servant "Whoever exalts himself [with haughtiness and empty pride] shall be humbled (brought low), and whoever humbles himself [whoever has a modest opinion of himself and behaves accordingly] shall be raised to honor" (AMP, Matthew 23:12) Christ's answer to the world's richest without Him; a man's life doesn't consist of the material possessions he accumulates, but his relationship toward God.

Even thousands of years after his death, Job's name is still associated with suffering and prosperity. Job suffered much evil at the hands of Satan. As a result, all of his children died instantly, his riches dissolved instantly, and his health diminished instantly. To add insult to injury, his wife questions, "Do you still hold fast your blameless uprightness? Renounce God and die!" (AMP, Job 2:9) Job responds, "You speak as one of the impious and foolish women would speak. What? Shall we accept [only] good at the hand of God and shall we not accept [also] misfortune and what is of a bad nature? In [spite of] all this, Job did not sin with his lips" (AMP, Job 2:9-10). After a period of time of testing and suffering, the Bible reveals, "And the Lord blessed the latter days of Job more than his beginning: for he had 14,000 sheep, 6,000 camels, 1,000 yoke of oxen, and 1,000 female donkeys. He had also seven sons and three daughters" (AMP, Job 42:12-13). The Lord gave him twice as much as he had before.

RECAP

Trying to make a name for yourself or allowing the world to put a name or label on you is not of God. Rather, it is of the world. The apostle Paul advises believers, "And my God will liberally supply (fill to the full) your every need according to His riches in glory in Christ Jesus"(AMP, Philippians 4:19). This provision includes spiritual and material needs. Young ladies and sisters in Christ, it is not the will of God that you strip in clubs for money to pay bills or to feed your children when Heaven is loaded! Young men and brothers in Chirst, that name you have been called because of your criminal background is not your real name! It is a negative name that tries to drive you to break the law. Who are you man of God? You came though your mother, but you came from God. The Bible states, "You were bought with a price [purchased with preciousness and paid for, made His own]. So then, honor God and bring glory to Him in your body" (AMP, 1 Corinthians 6:20). We are children of the light and not of darkness.

What's in a name? The Book of Ecclesiastes instructs, "A GOOD name is better than precious ointment; and the day of death than the day of one's birth" (KJV, 7:1). Solomon is suggesting, here, that it is better to come to the end of life with a good reputation (good name) than it is to have a joyful and auspicious beginning which, because of folly, might result in nothing.

DISCUSSION QUESTIONS

1. Why did the King of Babylon change Daniel and his friends' names?
2. What is the definition of personality?
3. In what developmental period do people generally discover their identities?
4. Define identity crises. How does identity crisis affect an individual's mentality and spirituality?
5. What are the odds of a rich unbeliever entering the Kingdom of God?
   a. Discuss Luke 18:24-25
6. What is mammon?
7. Is money the answer to everything?
   a. Discuss
8. Can a nickname drive someone to behave a certain way? Why or why not?
9. Is God against believers having material things? Discuss.

NOTES

CHAPTER 6

PURPOSE DRIVEN YOUNG PEOPLE

"But Daniel purposed in his heart that he would not defile himself with the portion of the king's meat, nor with the wine which he drank: therefore he requested of the prince of the eunuchs that he might not to defile himself" (KJV, Daniel 1:8).

The Hebrew word for purpose is siym [שׂים] meaning to place or put something on one's heart.

"The first thing in life is that of a purpose definitely recognized and accepted; and then acted upon. If that purpose be true, God is always in cooperation, and He is able to control circumstances in the interest thereof."[1] This reveals the secret of Daniel's success.

Daniel gave direction to his spiritual heart by refusing to contaminate his body, his mind, and his spirit with the King's food because they were sacrifice to idols. It is here Daniel takes a holy stance against King Nebuchadnezzar and the great Babylonian Empire. The King James Version of the previous verse says, "But Daniel purposed in his heart;" in other words, to deposit or put something on one's heart or mind for consideration. He was a young man of purpose and standard. "It was here that Daniel took his first stand. He was not exempt from temptation, but he refused to yield to that temptation. No man is of any use, nor will be ever of any use, if he is not a man of high purpose when faced with temptation to do wrong."[2]

---

1   G. Campbell Morgan, *Life Applications from Every Chapter of the Bible* (Grand Rapids, MI: Fleming H. Revell, 1994), 273.

2   Lehman Strauss, *The Prophecies of Daniel,* 1st ed (Grand Rapids, MI: Wm. B. Eardman's Publishing Company, 1969), 41.

DON'T FOLLOW YOUR HEART

"The heart is deceitful above all things, and desperately wicked: who can know it" (KJV, Jeremiah 17:9)?

Many people repeat the saying "follow your heart" when dealing with life's tough decisions; this saying my friends is contrary to what scriptures teach. The heart is more than just a physical organ needed to sustain life; it is the inner most part of one's being and the center of cravings, emotions, and the nucleus of the thought life. The secular way of thinking supports the idea that the human brain is the nucleus of human activity; however, the Bible reveals that the heart is the focal point of human activity. Case in point, the Book of Proverbs instructs, "Keep thy heart with all diligence; for out of it are the issues of life" (KJV, 4:23). The heart –the Hebrew noun leb, pronounced labe, [בל] — is used extensively for "the feelings, the will and even the intellect; likewise for the center of anything."[3] The Strong's Exhaustive Concordance defines the heart as not only the motives, feelings, affections, and desires; but also the will, the aims, the principles, the thoughts, and the intellect of man.[4] In fact, based on the Hebrew word "labe," the heart embraces the whole inner man, while the head was never being regarded as the seat of intelligence.

Countless numbers of people have followed their hearts and have ended up making terrible choices. The Book of Jeremiah makes it clear that "The heart is deceitful...desperately wicked: who can know it" (17:9). We do not even know our own hearts! For example, have you ever said "I would never do that?" yet as time lapse we end up doing what we said we will never do. This verse of scripture makes it clear that the human heart is deprave and cannot be changed by itself. The only solution to a dysfunctional heart is found in God and in His saving grace. He will give you a new heart after you have first surrendered it to Him through accepting His son Jesus Christ.

---

3   James Strong, *Strong's Expanded Exhaustive Concordance of the Bible* (Thomas Nelson Publisher, Nashville, TN, 2001), 129.
4   Ibid., 129.

HEART FUNCTIONS

Now that we have established the foundation of what the heart is in relation to decision making, what state the human heart is in, and how we can change that state through Christ Jesus, let me educate you on the two functions of the heart.

Function 1: The heart is the focal point of intellect. "For as he thinketh in his heart, so is he" (KJV, Proverbs 23:7a). This generally means that if you think you are a failure, you're going to act like a failure, talk like a failure, walk like a failure, hang around failures, and eventually become a failure. But if you think like a winner, talk like a winner, associate yourself with winners, behave like a winner, find out what winners have in common, then one will eventually take measures to become a winner.

Function 2: The heart is the core the human will. Paul states, "For with the heart a person believes (adheres to, trusts in, and relies on Christ) and so is justified (declared righteous, acceptable to God)"(AMP, Romans 10:10a). I believe that Daniel understood that the heart needs purpose (emotions), plans (intellect) and pursuit (human will) in order to make Godly decisions to take a stand.

BACK TO DANIEL...

What did Daniel have to guide him in this critical point in his life? Separated from his country and his family in a foreign land with its many gods, Daniel made one of the greatest decisions in his life as a teenager; living rightly before God. He possibly had the books of Genesis, Exodus, Leviticus, Numbers, Deuteronomy, and maybe inspired writings from David and some of the prophets before taken into captivity to help guide him. Young people of this generation — whether in college, high school, middle school, or elementary — face many important decisions. Unlike Daniel, we have the Old and New Testament as our compass in this ungodly culture to point us to Christ Jesus as our example.

We can only imagine Daniel reflecting about Moses in his dormitory-like facility making a choice in the Old Testament, as the Apostle Paul records in a snapshot —

- "Moses when he had grown to maturity and become great, by refusing to be called the son of Pharaoh's daughter" (AMP, Hebrews 11:24).

- "Because he [Moses] preferred to share the oppression [suffer the hardships] and bear the shame of the people of God rather than to have the fleeting enjoyment of a sinful life. He considered the contempt, abuse, and shame [borne for] the Christ (the Messiah who was to come) to be greater wealth than all the treasures of Egypt, for he looked forward and away to the reward (recompense). [Motivated] by faith, he left Egypt behind him, being unawed and dismayed by the wrath of the King: for he never flinched but held staunchly to the purpose and endured steadfastly as one who gazed on Him who is invisible" (AMP, Hebrews 11:25-27).

- Moses refused to be called son of Pharaoh's daughter (Hebrews 11:24).

Moses didn't want to and wouldn't have wanted to be associated with organizations and trends like secret societies, cults, crazes, occults, and gangs because of what they represented. Halloween, horoscopes, i-dosing, teen sex bracelets, teen toxing, smoking k2, sexting, fence plowing, and chat roulette, to name a few, are some modern-day examples of what Moses would have rejected. Just like Moses didn't want to be associated with these things, we too can refuse to partake in events, trends, and organizations that are harmful to our physical, mental, spiritual, and emotional beings.

Can you picture behind closed doors the conversations among Daniel and his peers? "Listen Daniel, we are a long way from home. Nobody will know or care what you do here. We are off here by ourselves." Another might have said, "Come on Daniel, it's just a little thing. It really doesn't matter." Another might have urged, "Now then, Daniel let's not get legalistic about this. You can carry that kind of thing too far." Somebody else might have commented, "Daniel everybody is doing it, plus how can we win people for God if we offend them?"[5] Although, there could have been internal pressure within him or peer pressure, the Bible records that Daniel determined in his heart that he would not

---

5   John Phillips and Jerry Vines, *Exploring the Book of Daniel* (Neptune, New Jersey: Loizeaux Brothers, 1999), 28.

defile himself. We must remember there could have been three hundred or more young boys, yet the Bible only speaks of four godly teenagers who stood up against the great Babylonian Empire, but in Daniel 1:8, he stands alone.

Daniel's desire was to please God first — not his culture, the society, or his peers/friends. In a post-modern culture that believes that right is wrong and wrong is right, there must be a standard for which young people are to live by if there is going to be success in this godless culture. This standard is the Word of the living God. Christ Jesus our Lord must become relevant to us. Wherever we are in life, Christs' instructions are clear. "But seek (aim at and strive after) first of all His Kingdom and His righteousness (His way of doing and being right), and then all these things taken together will be given you" (Matthew 6:33). Christ is saying:

- First search, inquire, study, and read about Christ and His Kingdom, which means seek, inquire, study, and read about God's way of doing things. What is God's way of doing things? The Bible records God's way of doing things — Philippians 2:12-13; Isaiah 66:2; Proverbs 3:7, 8:13; Matthew 5:10; and James 1-4.)

- Second, His righteousness means being in right standing with God and accepting salvation.

    "For it is by free grace (God's unmerited favor) that you are saved (delivered from judgment and made partakers of Christ's salvation) through [your] faith. And this [salvation] is not of yourselves [of your own doing, it come not through your own striving], but it is the gift of God" (AMP, Ephesians 2:8).

- Third, and all these things shall be added unto you. What things? The blessings of God are sure to follow you, if you follow God's order of seeking His face and getting to know Him because He loves you.

STAND STILL

"If a man hasn't discovered something he would die for, he isn't fit to live."

-Dr. Martin Luther King-

When was the last time you took a stand against Satan, the world, and your flesh? Paul says,

"Do you not know that being the world's friend is being God's enemy? So whoever chooses to be a friend of the world takes his stand as an enemy of God. Or do you suppose that the scripture is speaking to no purpose when it says, The Spirit whom He has caused to dwell in us yearns over us and He yearns for the Spirit [to be welcomed] with a jealous love?" (AMP, James 4:4b-7)

One illustration of being the "world's friend" is through spiritual infidelity, an unfaithfulness to Christ and His Word which includes sin and evil desires. That is why James says, "God sets Himself against the proud and haughty, but gives grace [continually] to the lowly (those who are humble enough to receive it)" (AMP, James 4:6). The holy scriptures instruct that we have the ability to resist the devil if we first submit to God. James 4:7 says: "**Submit** yourselves therefore to God. **Resist** the devil, and he will flee from you." The verb **submit** in the Greek language is (hupotasso) ὑποτασσω which originally was used as a military term meaning "to arrange [troop divisions] in a military fashion under the command of a leader."[6] The verb (submit) renders a continuous act of submitting to God presently — its perfect tense renders a completing action in the past that still gives us victory in the present and future. Victory attained by Christ on the cross and His resurrection. This is first done by listening, following, and obeying Christ and His Word. What a revelation! It is revealed that if you're submitting to God, you're in the army of the Lord with full benefits.

> *"But He gives us more and more grace (power of the Holy Spirit, to fully meet this evil tendency and all others)"* [Jer. 3:14; Hosea 2:19ff].

The verb **resist**, or *anthistemi*, [ανθίστημί] in Greek, "is in the perfect tense rendering a completing action in the past which means "to set in opposition, to oppose, and to stand against."[7] It is the will of God after

---

6   James Strong, *Strong's Expanded Exhaustive Concordance of the Bible* (Thomas Nelson Publisher, Nashville, TN, 2001), 260.

7   James Strong, *Strong's Expanded Exhaustive Concordance of the Bible* (Thomas Nelson Publisher, Nashville, TN, 2001), 26.

we have submitted to Christ to take a holy stand against the devil and his cohorts so they will flee. We must take a stand against illegal drugs, violence, premarital sex, drunkenness, theft, pornographic music, false religions, lying, skipping school, dropping out of school, selling drugs, gangs, etc. Choosing to follow Christ and His Word rather than the world's system of spiritual darkness and moral corruption is how we go about this. Praying to God in the name of Jesus for forgiveness of sins, being filled with the Holy Spirit, and joining a Bible believing church are the essentials you need to live a meaningful life called by Christ. I am reminded of one of many promises of God to believers:

> "But no weapon that is formed against you shall prosper, and every tongue that shall rise against you in judgment you shall show to be in the wrong. This [peace, righteousness, security, triumph over opposition] is the heritage of the servants of the Lord [those in whom the ideal servant of the Lord is reproduced]; this is the righteousness or vindication which they obtain from Me [this is that which I impart to them as their justification], says the Lord." (AMP, Isaiah 54:17)

Christ has your back! "For God did not give us a spirit of timidity (of cowardice, of craven and cringing fawning fear), but [He has given us a spirit] of power and of love and of calm and well-balanced mind and discipline and self-control." (AMP, 2 Timothy 1:7).

Fear is false evidence appearing real. Webster's Dictionary defines fear as "a torment, oppression, depression that causes paralysis, and an inability to move or feel." *Phobos* (the Greek word meaning terror, dread, and fear) is what God has already delivered us from. How? I'm glad you asked! According to the Book of 1 John, "There is no *phobos* [terror] in *agape* [love], but perfect *agape* [love] casteth out *phobos* [terror]: because phobos [terror] hath torment. He that feareth is not made perfect in love" (KJV, 4:18).

EXAMPLES OF PEOPLE STANDING UP

There are other people outside of Biblical records who have taken a holy stance against evil ideologies and empires. Recognized people such as politicians, statesmen, lawyers and activists, and even civil rights leaders have all rose to the height of humanity with sacrifice, bravery, and an undying will of fearless leadership. These people include:

SIR WINSTON CHURCHILL

Sir Winston Churchill was a British politician and statesman recognized for his fearless leadership and defiant stance during World War II against Nazi Germany and Adolf Hitler. The result of this refusal to surrender or compromise led to a rally of the British people who joined the Allied Forces in defeating Nazi Germany. Furthermore, Churchill is the only British prime minister to have received the Nobel Prize in Literature.[8]

NELSON MANDELA

Mr. Nelson Mandela was a lawyer and activist in South Africa who was incarcerated for 27 years because of his crusade against apartheid. After being released from prison in 1990, he later became his country's first black president, after being awarded the Nobel Peace Prize five months later. He unanimously won in South Africa first-time democratic elections in which all races voted.[9]

OSCAR SCHINDLER

"This is the true story of one remarkable man who outwitted Hitler and the Nazis to save more Jews from the gas chambers than any other during World War II."[10]

"Oscar Schindler rose to the highest level of humanity, walked through the bloody mud of the Holocaust without soiling his soul, his compassion, his respect for human life — and gave his Jews a second chance at life. He miraculously managed to do it and pulled it off by using the very same talents that made him a war profiteer — his flair presentation, bribery, and grand gestures."[11]

---

8   http://www.chu.cam.ac.uk/archives/collections/churchill_papers/biography/churchill_chronology.php

9   Ibid.

10   http://www.nelsonmandela.org/content/page/biography/

11   Ibid.

ROSA PARKS

Rosa Parks is called "the first lady of civil rights" and "the mother of the freedom movement," because of her refusal to follow a bus driver orders and give up her seat to a white passenger. This act of defiance against the powers that be, many say she ignited the Civil Rights Movement.[12]

PURPOSE DRIVEN YOUNG PEOPLE

Daniel and his friends are examples of purpose driven teens. Here is a list of purpose driven young people:

1. Mark Zukerberg — 21 years old, founded Facebook
2. Bill Gates — 19 years old, started the world's first microcomputer software company
3. Tim Berners-Lee — 24 years old, father of the World Wide Web developed hypertext links to connect information stored in different documents.
4. Langston Hughes was a poet, novelist, essayist, playwright, autobiographer, and writer of children's books. He published the poem "The Negro Speaks of Rivers" when he was 19.
5. Joseph — 17 years old, sold into slavery by his brothers, falsely accused of rape, received jail time for up to 3 years, God was with him. At the age of 30 he became second in all of Egypt (Genesis 14:40-57)
6. Mary — 16 years old (approximately), accepted the honor of becoming the mother of Jesus.
7. Tim Tebow — Heisman Trophy, Maxwell Award, MVP and 25th overall pick in the 2010 NFL Draft to the Denver Broncos.
8. AC Green — - Los Angeles Lakers
9. Dr. Benjamin Carson after medical school became a neurosurgery resident at the world famous John Hopkins Hospital in Baltimore. At age 32, he became the hospital's Director of Pediatric Neurosurgery.
10. Gabby Douglas: 16 years old, Olympic gold medalist

As you can see here, God uses purpose driven young people in very

---

12   www.wikipedia.com

unique ways because they took a step of faith. These many individuals have sent shock waves around the world that are still being felt decades later. I dare you to be like Daniel and friends!

DISCUSSION QUESTIONS

1. What does purpose driven mean?
2. What is the Hebrew word for heart?
   a. Why is it important not to trust my heart?
3. What are the two functions of the heart?
4. Name one biblical purpose driven teen in either the Old/New Testament. Give a description of how they were purpose driven.
5. Explain Jeremiah 17:9.
6. What does "submit" mean in James 4:7?
7. What does "resist" mean in James 4:7?

NOTES

CHAPTER 7

I WILL NOT DEFILE MYSELF

"But Daniel determined in his heart that he would not defile himself by [eating his portion of] the king's rich and dainty food or by [drinking] the wine which he drank; therefore he requested of the chief of the eunuchs that he might [be allowed] not to defile himself" (AMP, Daniel 1:8b).

THE PROBLEM

"The command of the King was that the young men be fed with the food and wine from the King's table, was to Daniel and his friends a test of their fidelity to the Lord and to His Law, like that to which Joseph was subjected in Egypt, corresponding to the circumstances in which he was placed, of his fidelity to God (Gen. 39:7). The partaking of the food brought to them from the king's table was to them contaminating, because forbidden by Law; not so much because the food was not prepared according to the Levitical ordinance, or perhaps consisted of the flesh of animals which to the Israelites were unclean, but the reason of their rejection of it was that the heathen at their feasts offered up in sacrifice to their gods, a part of the food and the drink, and thus consecrated their meals by a religious right; whereby not only he who participated in such a meal participated in the worship of idols, but the meat and the wine as a whole were the meat and the wine of an idol sacrifice, partaking of which, according to the saying of the apostle (1 Cor. 10:20), is the same as sacrificing to devils."[1]

Daniel and his friends took a holy stand against the partaking of food and wine offered to idols, thus demonstrating qualities of young godly

---

1   Carl Friedrich Keil, *Biblical Commentary on the Book of Daniel*, trans. M.G. Easton. (Grand Rapids: Eardmans, 1955), 539-540.

men of purpose and morals. Their request not to defile themselves proves that as believers "a soft answer turns away wrath" (AMP, Proverbs 15:1), and that unbelievers are changed many times not by what we say, but how we behave. The Christian character is what defines a person of purpose. A person will only go as far as their character will take them.

Although today we are under the New Covenant, the principle still remains: don't eat food or drink the sacrifices made to idols. Provided below is a table that gives a description of the differences between the Mosaic and the New Covenant.

	MOSAIC COVENANT	NEW COVENANT
View of the Mosaic/New Covenant	For Israel only to obey (Exodus 19:5; Deuteronomy 5:1-21)	Jewish Believers and Believers are not required to follow the Law of Moses. (Romans 6:14,8:3-4) For all who partake in the New Covenant through Jesus Christ accepts its blessings and salvation by faith/ obedience. (Heb.8:6)[2] Gal. 3:23-25.
Relationship & Nature	Was temporary and conditional. Rom. 10:4; Gal. 3:19-29; Eph. 2:11-18. But not the Old Testament.	Unconditional and Eternal (Romans 15:4) Rom. 4:15, 5:19-21, 7:7-14; Gal. 3:19
Sanctification	Law written on stone tablets	Law written on human hearts. (Jeremiah 31:31-34) "they shall all know me"

---

2   Donald C. Stamps, ed., *The Full Life Study Bible* (Grand Rapids, MI: Zondervan Publishing House, 1992), 1955.

	MOSAIC COVENANT	NEW COVENANT
View of Self	Unregenerate and can't keep the Law.	Saved by grace through faith in Jesus Christ. (Ephesians 2:8)
Origin	From the exodus to the cross[3]	From resurrection to eternity.[4]
Meat	Forbidden— Deuteronomy 14:4-6,9,11,20 Permitted— Deuteronomy 14:7-8, 10,12-19	All meat allowed to eat. Acts 10:11-16; Mark 7:18-23; Colossians 2:14-16
Alcoholic Drinks	Priests & Nazarites abstained from alcohol during time of ministry (Leviticus 10:9-11; Numbers 6:3)	Drunkards will not inherit the kingdom of God. 1 Corinthians 6:9-10
Foods offered to idols	The Book of Leviticus forbids foods offered to idols.	Believers are forbidden to eat food offered to idols. 1 Corinthians 8:1-13, Acts 21:25

The Apostle Paul states:

"No, I am suggesting that what the pagans sacrifice they offer [in effect] to demons (to evil spiritual powers) and not to God [at all]. I do not want you to fellowship and be partners with diabolical spirits [by eating at their feasts]. You cannot drink the Lord's cup and the demon's cup. You cannot partake of the Lord's table and the demon's table." (AMP, 1 Corinthians 10:20-21)

It is obvious to most Christians that idolatry includes the worship of

---

3   J. E. Harttill, *Principles of Biblical Hermeneutics* (Grand Rapids, MI: Zondervan Publishing House, 1947), 14.

4   Ibid., 25.

demons and connections with all sorts of evil. However, what is not obvious to most believers (as well as young people) is that demonic powers stand behind love for worldly possessions, power, and reputation. Today's youth are offered these worldly possessions, power, and fame in the form of sacrifices from Satan's table of delicacies. For many people these temptations are just material belongings, but to the enemy of our faith, they are sacrifices! Webster's Dictionary defines sacrifice as a practice of offering something, to up something of value for something else. An example of a sacrifice would be when people exchange Christ for worldly things. Jesus asks, "For what will it profit a man if he gains the whole world and forfeits his life [his blessed life in the Kingdom of God]" (AMP, Matthew 16:26)? Or what would a man give as an exchange for his [blessed] life [in the Kingdom of God]?

The Bible brings to light many of these diabolical sacrifices, so that we as believers may become aware, come out from among them, and be saved and set free to live for the Lord. The apostle states:

> "But understand this, that in the last days will come (set in) perilous times of great stress and trouble [hard to deal with and hard to bear]. For people will be lovers of self and [utterly] self-centered, lovers of money and aroused by an inordinate [greedy] desire for wealth, proud and arrogant and contemptuous boasters. They will be abusive (blasphemous, scoffing), disobedient to parent, ungrateful, unholy and profane. [They will be] without natural [human affection (callous and inhuman), relentless (admitting of no truce or appeasement); [they will be] slanderers (false accusers, trouble makers), intemperate and loose in morals and conduct, uncontrolled and fierce, haters of good. [They will be] treacherous [betrayers], rash, [and] inflated with self-conceit. [They will be] lovers of sensual pleasures and vain amusements more than and rather than lovers of God. For [although] they hold a form of piety (true religion), they deny and reject and are strangers to the power of it [their conduct belies the genuineness of their profession]. Avoid [all] such people [turn away from them]. For among them are those who worm their way into homes and captivate silly and weak-natured and spiritually dwarfed women, loaded

down with [the burden of their] sins [and easily] swayed and led away by various evil desires and seductive impulses." (AMP, II Timothy 3:1-6)

In other words, lust of the eyes make material things seem like a life luxury that one can't live without (fast and illegal money schemes, selling drugs, adultery, gambling, stealing, rape, credit card fraud, etc.) but these provisions and illusions from the god of this world doesn't meet the requirements of the Word of God because it violates the holy scriptures. These evil delecacies are like junk-food to the body and soul; providing no nutrition or good to the body only shortening life little by little. How? It creates a fantasy through the creative imagination, an unrealistic mental image in response to a spiritual need. It temporarily appears that these desires are full and met, but there is one problem; it's not real. That's the great deception of Satan and his world table of delicacies. The good news is that while you're alive now you can denounce these satanic appetites, asks for forgiveness, and live for Christ Jesus our Lord.

DRUNKENNESS
IS IT OKAY TO GET DRUNK?

I have had the opportunity to work with young people ages of 16-24 for about 20 years and there are two questions they frequently ask me that I will attempt to answer. First — is it forbidden to drink intoxicating wine? Second — is it a sin to get drunk?

First, the Bible in the Old Testament has four different Hebrew names for wine: yayin (used 140xs), tiyrosh (used 38xs), chamar (used 6xs), and mamcak (used once). I will elaborate on each one and hopefully provide some clarity on the subject of drinking.

Yayin is the most common name for wine, basically known as fermented or intoxicating wine and unfermented grape juice wine. "The Bible first describes the evil effects of intoxicating wine in the story of Noah (Genesis 9:20-27). He planted a vineyard, harvested it, made intoxicating wine from the grapes, and drank from it. Doing so led to drunkenness, immodesty, indiscretion, and the family tragedy of a curse placed on Canaan. The Book of Genesis describes the effects of alcohol on Noah "And Noah awoke from his wine (yayin), and knew what his younger son had done unto him" (9:24).[5] One act of indiscretion not only affects you, but your family, and those around you. Also, the damaging effects of intoxicating wine (yayin) were felt at the time of Abraham.

"Intoxicating wine was the culprit that led to incest and to the pregnancies of Lot's daughters" (AMP, Genesis 19:31-38)."[6] I can recall a former student of mine that nearly obtained a perfect score on the GED test, but was terminated from the program for being drunk. How many stories have we heard of when young ladies got drunk and the results were nothing less of terrible (contraction of STI's, children out of wedlock, fatal car wrecks, and even rape). Furthermore, "Because of the corrupting potential of alcoholic drinks, God commanded all priests of Israel to abstain from all types of wine and strong drink during their time of ministry unto Him. God regarded the violation of this command sufficiently serious to warrant the death penalty for the offending priest (Leviticus 10:9-11)."[7] In the New Testament, the Bible describes all believers as a "chosen generation, a royal priesthood, a holy nation, a peculiar people"(KJV, 1 Peter 2:9a). How much is expected of us today as we minister to our Lord? We too should abstain from wine (yayin), knowing it will result in us only becoming a stumbling block to believers and unbelievers alike. Scripture supports this claim in "Abstain from all appearance of evil" (KJV, 1 Thessalonians 5:22). "God also revealed His will concerning wine and strong drink by making abstinence a requirement for all who took the Nasserite vow."[8] One of the famous Nasserites found in scripture is Samson. Known for his strength and fighting ability, God appointed him as judge and he began to deliver Israel out of the Land of the Philistines.

---

5   Donald C. Stamps, ed. ,*The Full Life Study Bible* (Grand Rapids, MI: Zondervan Publishing House, 1992), 220-221.

6   Ibid.

7   Ibid.

8   Ibid.

The angel instructs Samson's mother, "Drink not wine nor strong drink, and eat not any unclean thing because your son shall be a Nasserite unto God from the womb" (KJV, Judges 13:7). The Jewish Encyclopedia explains there were two reasons for the Nasserite vow — dedication to God and to atone for sins and healing. "Solomon's God-given wisdom led him to write: "Wine is a mocker, strong drink is raging: and whosoever is deceived thereby is not wise" (KJV, Proverbs 20:1, note). Alcoholic beverages can cause one to mock God's standard of righteousness and to lose self-control with regard to sin and immorality."[9] When people are under the influence of alcohol (or any other substance) they lose the ability to make wise decisions.

"Finally, the scriptures unequivocally state that in order to avoid woe and sorrow and instead to follow God's will, the righteous must not even look upon or desire any fermented wine that can intoxicate and cause addiction"[10] (KJV, Proverbs 23:29-35). Needless to say, I often tell my students not to adopt unexpected evil thoughts that bombard them by Satan, neither allow them to condemn you or place you in bondage. Christ doesn't condemn every thought that invades our minds; rather He condemns evil thoughts acted upon. This is supported in scripture where Jesus was teaching His disciples and the multitudes of people about looking and lusting after a woman and how this constitutes as adultery (Matthew 5:28).

"Did Jesus use fermented or unfermented grape drink when He instituted the Lord's Supper (Matthew 26:26-29; Mark 14:22-25; Luke 22:17-20; 1 Corinthians 11:23-26)? The following data supports the conclusion that what Jesus and His disciples drank was unfermented grape juice."[11]

1. "Neither Luke nor any other Biblical writer uses the word 'wine' (Gk. Oinos) in regard to the Lord's Supper. The first three Gospel writers use 'fruit of the vine' (Matthew 26:29; Mark 14:25; Luke 22:18). Unfermented wine is the only true natural 'fruit of the vine', containing approximately 20% sugar and no alcohol. Fermentation destroys much of the sugar and alters what the

---

9   Ibid., 221.
10   Ibid.
11   Ibid., 1539.

vine produced. Fermented wine is not a product of the vine."[12]

2. "The Lord's Supper was instituted when Jesus and His disciples were eating for the Passover. The Passover law in Exodus 12:14-20 prohibited, during Passover week, the presence and use of seor (Exodus 12:15), a word referring to leaven, yeast, or any agent of fermentation. Seor in the ancient world was often obtained from the thick scum on top of fermenting wine. Furthermore, all hametz (i.e., anything contaminating any fermentation) was forbidding (Exodus 12:19; 13:7; see 13:7 note). God had given these laws because fermentation symbolized corruption and sin (cf. Matthew 16:6, 12:1; 1 Corinthians 5:7-8). Jesus, the Son of God, fulfilled the Law in every requirement (Matthew 5:17). Thus, He would have followed God's law for the Passover and not used fermented wine."[13]

3. A rather lively debate has taken place over the centuries among Jewish rabbis and scholars as to whether fermented products of the vine were allowed in the Passover. Those who held to a stricter and more literal interpretation of the Hebrew scriptures, especially Exodus 13:7, insisted that no fermented wine was to be used on this occasion."[14]

Second, is it a sin to get drunk? The Bible Dictionary describes drunkenness as a state of dizziness, headaches, and vomiting resulting from drinking alcoholic beverages. From Genesis 9:21 on, the Bible describes the shameful state of the drunken person and the shameful actions resulting from the state. Too much partying led to drunkenness and failure of communication between husband and wife (1 Samuel 25:36). It left a person defenseless against enemies (1 Kings 16:9-10, 20: 16). They sang loud songs ridiculing other people (Psalms 69:12) and could not walk straight (Job 12:25; Psalms 107:27). They vomited (Jeremiah 25:27) and were in a daze unaware of events around them (Joel 1:5). They ruined their future

COOL FACT

The Bible endorses abstaining from alcohol (Numbers 6:2-4; Jeremiah 35:1-19)

---

12 Ibid.
13 Ibid.
14 Ibid.

(Proverbs 23:20-21). They could not protect themselves against injuries such as avoiding a thorn bush (Proverbs 26:9). Drunken leaders ruin a nation (Isaiah 28:1-9). Being drunk became a figure of speech for having to drink the disaster God was sending (Isaiah 49:26). Drunkenness is a pagan custom, not a Christian one (1 Peter 4:3). Drunkards among those who will not "inherit the Kingdom of God" (1 Corinthians 6:10). Yes! "Drunkenness is a sin because it defiles your temple (1 Corinthians 6:19)."[15]

Sobriety is an issue that God cares about deeply for His people. Being sober-minded allows you to be free from addiction, able to be used by God, and improves your chances of a healthier relationship with family and friends.

DISCUSSION QUESTIONS

1. Can Christians drink alcohol?
2. What type of wine did Christ and his disciples drink? Fruit of the vine or intoxicating wine? Explain.
3. What are the Hebrew names for wine?
4. What does 1 Corinthians 6:10 say?
5. Under the New Covenant are believers require to follow the law?
   a. List scriptural proof

---

15   Trent C. Butler, *Holeman Bible Dictionary* (Nashville, Tennessee: Holeman Bible Publisers, 1991), 380.

NOTES

CHAPTER 8

DIVINE FAVOR & TENDER LOVE

"Now God made Daniel to find favor, compassion, and loving kindness with the chief of the eunuchs" (AMP, Daniel 1:9).

The favor of God renders mercy, kindness, unfailing love, and faithfulness. God gave Daniel divine favor with the prince of the eunuchs, which was evidence that the eunuch's heart was changed. Daniel walked in divine favor because he pleased God. Enoch is an example of one who pleased God. Found in Hebrews 11:5 — "Because of faith Enoch was caught up and transferred to heaven, so the he did not have a glimpse of death; and he was not found, because God had translated him. For even before he was taken to heaven, he received testimony [still on record] that he pleased and been satisfactory to God." As we break it down to the lowest common denominator, we will see that favor come by simply pleasing God.

Let's investigate the life of Enoch to see what it is to please God and what is meant by finding favor. The Bible records, "Enoch walked [in habitual fellowship] with God after the birth of Methuselah 300 years and had other sons and daughters" (AMP, Genesis 5:22). The first thing implied in Enoch's walk with God is reconciliation. A pertinent question is asked in Amos 3:3:

> How can two walk together except they be agreed? Thus two walking together supposes agreement, sympathy, and harmony. From the nature of the case, it is implied that one of the two had been at enmity with the other and that there had been reconciliation. So that when we say of any man that he walks with God, it implies that he has been reconciled to God.

To walk with God implies a correspondency of nature. Light hath no communion with darkness. No sinner can walk with God for he has nothing in common with Him, and more, his mind is at enmity against Him. It is sin which separates from God. The day that Adam sinned, he fled from his maker and hid himself among the trees of the Garden. A walk with God then supposes the judicial putting away of sin and the impartation of the divine nature to the one who walked with Him. In a sentence, the walking with God means that we cease taking our own way, that we abandon the world's way, that we follow the divine way. To walk with God implies a surrendered will."[1]

Daniel like Enoch had faith in God, which pleased God and gave him favor with God. Now let's look at the heroes of faith that found favor with God.

Daniel like Enoch had faith in God, which pleased God and gave him favor with God. Now let's look at five examples of the heroes' of the faith and how they found favor with God.

First, **Sarah the wife of Abraham a recipient of God's favor to do the impossible** in her elderly years because she believed the promised of God at the age of ninety, and Abraham at the age one hundred years old for bearing a son. Sarah name means "princess" the "mother of nations." Sarah laughed at the promise of God when she first heard it possibly making sport of it, but a year later after her promised son was born she laughed in pleasure at the favor God bestowed on her. Sarah found favor with God for the impossible, her body being aged, yet alive with the ability to give birth from the promised of God. God's response to her laughing the very first time was, "Is anything too hard for the Lord?" This is the question we must ask ourselves when facing impossible odds, like Sarah we might laugh, yet persevere in faith and believed God to be a recipient of God's favor to do the impossible. (*KJV*, Hebrews 11:11)

Second, **Rahab the prostitute found favor with God for deliverance**

---

1   John Philips and Jerry Vines, *Exploring the Book of Daniel.* (United States: Loizeaux Brothers Inc. 1990) 50.

for her household and family's household, because she hid the two Hebrews spies in Jericho who came there to survey the land of Jericho from the king. (Joshua 2) She was a harlot with a pagan background who feared/reverenced the God of Israel and recognized Him as the God of Heaven. She made a vow with the spies for them to spare her family's life when they come back to destroy Jericho. Rahab deserted the pagan gods and accepted the True and Living God. Amazingly many people are shocked that she's included with the heroes of faith in Hebrews chapter 11 along with Abraham, Jacob, Isaac, Gideon, David and many others. Furthermore, she's mentioned in the ancestry of Christ in the Book of Matthew. This is a true reminder of the favor of God and how He used the "least of these," as He told Moses "I have mercy on whom I have mercy, and I have compassion on whom I have compassion." (Romans, 9:15 NIV) Just like Rahab, Daniel found favor in pagan countries and you too can have the favor of God in your life by trusting and believing in Christ even in impossible situations.

Third, **Joseph in the Old Testament found favor with God for promotion.** Joseph was one of the youngest sons of Jacob and Rachael, eleventh of twelve brothers. He received "a coat of many colors" from his father Jacob, and is considered as one of his favorite sons. This gift created jealousy and envy among the other brothers, along with his prophetic dream of ruling over his family, who immediately sold Joseph out to some strangers. Joseph was taken to Egypt and became a slave to one of Pharaoh's officers, whose wife accused him of rape, after he resisted her advances, ran away, and was thrown into prison. While in prison he interpreted a few dreams from the king of Egypt's butler and baker who offended him. Later, Pharaoh the king of Egypt, had a troublesome dream that needed interpretation and he heard about Joseph who was brought before the king from prison for interpretation of his dream. Joseph interprets Pharaoh's dream and what the Lord was going to do to Egypt, he predicted seven years of abundance and seven years of shortage. Pharaoh couldn't find anyone as wise as Joseph in this matter, so he made him second in command in all of Egypt to govern his affairs. This is the favor of God who promoted Joseph despite his brothers selling him out, a false accusation of rape, and imprisonment, Joseph now became second in command in all of Egypt. We must remember Joseph was 17years old when he was sold into slavery, and at the age of 30 years old he stood in a position of honor in all of Egypt. (Genesis 36:1 — 47:26) (Hebrews 11:22)

Fourth, **David found favor with God and was chosen as the second human king of Israel.** The reason I put emphasis on "human king" because God is the first King of Israel. (Psalm 5:2) Saul the first human king of Israel was rejected by God because of his disobedience and rebellion. God sent the prophet Samuel to anoint a new king in Bethlehem among the sons of Jessie. Samuel begun to call forth Jessie's son's to pass in front of him, so seven of his son's pass before Samuel, I can imagine because they were in Israel's army, they probably looked like NFL football players, bodybuilders, hockey players or candidates for the Olympics. As the first son pass before Samuel, he looked at him and said "Surely the Lord's anointed is before him." But the Lord corrected his prophet Samuel and said "Look not on his countenance or on the height of his stature; because I have refused him: for the Lord seeth not as man seeth; *for man looketh on the outward appearance, but the Lord looketh on the heart."*(KJV, 1 Samuel 16:7) This is a lesson for many leaders in the church choosing someone for a leadership position; we must stop looking at who has the most money, talents, credentials or degrees — focus our attention on the number one prerequisite God reveals "the heart." Back to Samuel who then asked all of Jessie's son to pass before him, again God rejected all of his sons it appears. Now Samuel the Prophet is baffled, and asked Jessie is this all of your children. Jessie responded, there is one more the youngest, he's a sheep herder. I can imagine the prophet is excited, the father is excited and the people are excited. Who is this teenager, God has chosen to be king of Israel? The bible describes teenage David as "a healthy reddish complexion and

COOL FACTS

Did you know David was a talented Psalmist and fierce warrior? for the Lord?

beautiful eyes, and was fine looking." (AMP, 1 Samuel 16:12) Next, God informed Samuel to rise an anoint David as king. Although, David didn't become king two years later, it's remarkable to see how God's chooses versus how a person chooses. David found favor with God and was chosen to be king because of his heart. Young people if you want favor with God, be like teenage David who developed a heart and hunger for God. (1 Samuel 16:1-22) (Hebrews 11:32)

Fifth, **the three Hebrew boys found favor with God for supernatural deliverance in the midst of a fiery furnace.** Nebuchadnezzar, the King of Babylon in Daniel chapter 3 made an image of Gold and gathers his officials and administrators together for a dedication and worship of the image. It is said the image of gold was of a man and represented king Nebuchadnezzar, ninety feet high and nine feet wide, truly an enormous statue. "What we are reading about here is an ancient version of what we might call today secular humanism, the attempt to deify man, the belief that man can solve all his problems." (Vines/Phillips – Daniel pg. 50) Next the king sent a messenger (false teacher/prophet) and commanded all of the people — who represent the many nations and languages — to fall down and worship the golden image when they hear different types of music. Today we must remember the biblical account of Genesis "man was made in image of God,"(KJV, Genesis 1:26) not the image of icon's, diva's, idols, entertainers, athletes, folk heroes, legends, billionaires, false prophets, music/pop stars, secret societies, and false god's. In this millennium we're losing too many of our young people who are worshiping images and who are being influenced by pornographic music, they must look back to examples in the bible, as well as look forward to their living examples like fathers, mothers, pastors, teachers and bible study teachers. In Daniel 3:6, the king sent word that "whosoever doesn't bow down and worship the image along with the music would be thrown in a burning fiery furnace." When living right for Christ it seems as if you always have some people looking for something to accuse you of. Well the three Hebrews boys were no different, the Chaldeans accused the Jews of not bowing to the image decreed from the king. The king of Babylon heard about the three Hebrews boys not bowing to his image and became outraged and commanded them to be brought before him. Nebuchadnezzar questioned the youths about their act of defiance; let's listen in on their conversation —

> "Nebuchadnezzar said unto them, Is it true, O Shadrach, Meshach, and Abed-nego, do not you serve my gods, nor worship the golden image which I have set up? Shadrach, Meshach, and Abed-nego, answered and said to the king, O Nebuchadnezzar, we are not careful to answer thee in this matter. If it be so, our God whom we serve is able to deliver us from the burning fiery furnace, and he will deliver us out of thine hand, O king. But if not, be it known unto thee, O king, that we will not serve thy gods, nor worship the golden image which thou hast set up." (KJV, Daniel 3:14, 16-18)(AMP, Hebrews 11:32)

Let this be a lesson to you going against what's popular or the crowd for the truth of God's Word. It's not easy being in middle school, high school, home school, college, or alternative school, taking a stand but you must not doubt standing for Christ and don't bow down to secular culture. Finally, the king of Babylon in all his fury commanded his soldiers to throw the Hebrews into the fiery furnace, because they refused to bow down to the image. They were bound in their clothes and thrown into the furnace; this oven was so hot that the soldiers even died in the process of throwing them in. Well the king decided to take a look inside the fiery furnace and instead of seeing three bound in the oven, he saw four. (KJV, Daniel 3: 19-25) God sent an angel or Christ Himself in that furnace with the Hebrew boys. That's the favor of God for supernatural deliverance! The Hebrews boys were not burned, nor did their clothes smell like fire. (KJV, Daniel 3:27-30) Keep this in mind in chapter four the meaning of Daniel's and Hananiah's name before it was change was "God is my judge," and Hananiah means "Yahweh has been gracious." What a revelation! God was their final Judge and He was gracious to them. (NIV, Daniel 1:7) Compromise is the battle ground, like the Hebrews be true to God and He will always be True to you.

God does not break the law; He works within our system of justice to accomplish His will.

Today young men and women can also walk in the favor of God, against a pagan culture like Babylon. You can have favor in college, the armed forces, on the job, in church, in a courtroom, in sports, when purchasing a home, while in jail/prison, while in school, when purchasing a home or car, etc. Many people might say,

- I am not Jewish, African-American/ European-American
- I come from a dysfunctional family
- I am not a great speaker
- I am overweight/underweight
- I don't look like "model material" or sing like the angels in heaven
- I am not good at sports or the most intelligent in my class

Here's the good news child of God, "For God shows no partiality [undue favor or unfairness; with Him one man is not different from another]." (AMP, Romans 2:11). We must remember God doesn't require ability, but He requires availability in order for us to be used. Christ will give you ability, intellect, and all sorts of gifts; however He desires time with you. Beloved you can too believe God and walk in these five benefits of divine favor into your life now.

DISCUSSION QUESTIONS

1. What does the favor of God render?
2. List a few of the favors provided. Support answers with scripture.
3. Name some biblical characters that walked in the favor of God.
4. How can I walk in the favor of God?
5. What are some benefits of walking in God's favor?

NOTES

CHAPTER 9

THE RESULTS OF TEENAGE FASTING
AND CULTURAL PARADIGMS

"Then compare our appearance with that of the young men who eat the royal food, and treat your servants in accordance with what you see" (NIV, Daniel 1:13).

"So he agreed to this and tested them for ten days. At the end of the ten days they looked healthier and better nourished than any of the young men who ate the royal food. So the guard took away their choice food and the wine they drink and gave them vegetables instead" (NIV, Daniel 1:14-16).

> *"So then, those who suffer according to God's will should commit themselves to their faithful Creator and continue to do good" (1 Peter 4:19).*

In the Book of Daniel the result is victory; exactly what one might expect it to be (NIV, 1:14). Following God's will regardless of the trial, test, difficulty or man's opinion will always turn out to be blessing. Although it may not look or feel like victory, it is victory because of God's Sovereignty (God is the source of creation) and faithfulness. God's faithfulness means that God will always do what He has said and fulfill what He has promised. As a youth in Sunday school my teacher would often say "God is everywhere present," expressing His Omnipresence. Daniel and his friends understood God's Sovereignty, faithfulness and His will, so that's why they trusted Him with the results of their trial in a life and death struggle for survival against the great Babylonian Empire. Well the results are that Daniel and his friends are healthier and looked better than the other young men that ate from this pagan king's table, rather than the King of Kings table; doing this will leave the believer wanting nothing. "The believer who adheres to the will of God shall not be found wanting." So the steward took away [rich] dainties and the wine they were to drink and gave them vegetables. (AMP, Daniel 1:16) Young people, use this story as an example to apply to your lives when considering diet and faith because Jesus wants you healthy and looking good because your body is the temple of the Holy Spirit (AMP, 1 Corinthians 6:19), so eat those healthy foods mentioned in chapter four and remain strong.

What a testimony to those Babylonian leaders of the power of Israel's God!

The spiritual significance of Daniel 1:14 is that although Daniel suggested the test, God permits or allows testing in the fire and through trials to strengthen us. Peter encourages us to embrace trials as an avenue for a closer walk with Christ:

> *"Dear friend, don't be bewildered or surprised when you go through the fiery trials ahead, for this is no strange, unusual thing that is going to happen to you. Instead be really glad because these trials will make you partners with Christ in his suffering and afterwards you will have the wonderful joy of sharing his glory in that coming day when it will be displayed"* (AMP, 1 Peter 4:12-14)

Although it may be hurtful and even disrespectful, be joyful if you are insulted for being a Christian. When that happens, the Spirit of God will come upon you with great glory and provide you strength in weakness to endure life's hardships. Tests come to take away your confidence in the flesh which in turn brings you closer to God, so you can rely less on your human strength and abilities and more on Him. In other words, sometimes you must fail tests to see your own limitations in order to pass God's test to see His grace.

DON'T WORRY, TRUST GOD!

"Worry is putting question marks where God has put periods."
~John R. Rice[1]

---

1   Robert Morgan, *Stories, Illustrations, and Quotes*, Thomas Nelson Publishers, Nashville, 2000 pg. 801

Daniel and friends exchanged worry for trusting in God. Worry is a byproduct of fear and of not trusting in God. Jesus taught against worry and fear throughout scripture. When Jesus preached the Sermon on the Mount, He commanded His hearers not to worry about tomorrow:

"For this reason I say to you, do not be worried about your life, as to what you will eat or what you will drink; nor for your body, as to what you will put on. Is not life more than food, and the body more than clothing? "Look at the birds of the air, that they do not sow, nor reap nor gather into barns, and yet your heavenly Father feeds them. Are you not worth much more than they? "And who of you by being worried can add a single hour to his life? "And why are you worried about clothing? Observe how the lilies of the field grow; they do not toil nor do they spin, yet I say to you that not even Solomon in all his glory clothed himself like one of these. "But if God so clothes the grass of the field, which is alive today and tomorrow is thrown into the furnace, will He not much more clothe you? You of little faith! "Do not worry then, saying, 'What will we eat?' or 'What will we drink?' or 'What will we wear for clothing?' "For the Gentiles eagerly seek all these things; for your heavenly Father knows that you need all these things. "But seek first His kingdom and His righteousness, and all these things will be added to you. "So do not worry about tomorrow; for tomorrow will care for itself. Each day has enough trouble of its own. (NAS, Matthew 6:25-34)

The God of creation doesn't want His children to worry about the basic necessities of life, because He created the heaven and the earth, and He's more than able to sustain and provide for His creation including you.

CULTURAL PARADIGMS

Let's look at cultural paradigms in schools, a place where various perceptions are derived. How people view life through their senses makes the difference on how they behave. To some, it doesn't make a difference whether their perceptions are good, bad, right, wrong, healthy, or unhealthy; what they see through their "eyegate," hear through their "eargate," or smell through their "nosegate" determines their behavior. Their mentality might be, "If it feels right, let's do it!" But there is only one problem, PEOPLE DON'T HAVE TO BE A PRODUCT OF THEIR ENVIRONMENTS. Life is about choices. Here is a list of paradigms some have about themselves and others that will affect their future.

PEER PRESSURE CENTERED

Many teenagers view their lives through the scope of their peers. If their peers are wearing the latest fashions, they must wear the latest fashions. If their friends are popular as a result of committing some careless act, they may feel pressured to commit this act in order to be a part of the in-crowd. This paradigm is dangerous because the center of the universe for these teens is their peers, who, frequently, do not have their best interests in mind nor do they view life from a biblical worldview. For example, in order to be part of a desired group, a girl may be pressured to engage in sexual activities with the popular guys in school. Not only is this risky act a sin, it may be against everything the girl has been taught from the Bible and her family. Teens should not base their identities on peers — who many times are fake, jealous, and immature. How do you know if your peers are the center of your life? You can tell when you are compelled to do everything they do, whether good or bad and regardless of the circumstances. That is just too much power to give to people who do not truly care about you!

SELF-CENTERED

Me, myself, and I is the only concern in life within this paradigm. Sometimes teens see the world through the reflection of a mirror. How do you know when you are self-centered? Answer: You have an **"I"** mentality. For example, you may think to yourself: I don't need my parents, I don't need a teacher, I don't need help in school, I don't need God or church. This is self-centered pride.

In the Book of Ezekiel, God's response to the prince of Tyrus' self-centered pride is recorded:

> *The word of the LORD came to me: "Son of man, say to the ruler of Tyre, 'This is what the Sovereign LORD says: " 'In the pride of your heart you say, "I am a god; I sit on the throne of a god*

in the heart of the seas." But you are a mere mortal and not a god, though you think you are as wise as a god. Are you wiser than Daniel? Is no secret hidden from you? By your wisdom and understanding you have gained wealth for yourself and amassed gold and silver in your treasuries. By your great skill in trading you have increased your wealth, and because of your wealth your heart has grown proud." 'Therefore this is what the Sovereign LORD says:" 'Because you think you are wise, as wise as a god, I am going to bring foreigners against you, the most ruthless of nations; they will draw their swords against your beauty and wisdom and pierce your shining splendor (NIV, 28:1-7).

God pronounced judgment against the Prince of Tyrus because of his prideful heart and looks. It is a reminder that "Pride goes before destruction, a haughty spirit before a fall." (NIV, Proverbs 16:18)

CULTURE CENTERED

The Webster's Dictionary defines culture as a form of civilization, beliefs, arts, and customs. For many years, I have worked in Miami, Florida — a large melting pot for numerous races, religions, and cultures. In this part of the country, people are proud of where they come from. As a result, they display flags, wear T-shirts, eat food, and listen to music that reflects the love they have for their cultural heritage. When culture becomes the center of your life, though, you are in danger of violating Scripture! If your culture interferes with going to school or church, being a gainfully employed, or acting as a law abiding citizen, you have a destructive culture. I have ministered to many young people who have put culture over Christ Jesus (which is a violation of the First Commandment — you must not have any other god before me). How do you know if you're culture centered? Answer: When you eat, sleep, and breathe culture, rather than the living whole-heartedly for God.

DRUGS CENTERED

In the Book of Genesis, God gives man "dominion" over the Earth (Chapter 1). The Bible does not say that God has given plants dominion over man. If drugs, like marijuana and cocaine, are your center, then plants dictate your life. How crazy does that sound? A plant nourished by horse manure has control over you! For instance, cocaine in its altered state — crack — has destroyed many families, lives, and careers. Studies have proven that marijuana kills brain cells as well as causes different types of cancer. I am not referring to marijuana that is legally prescribed by doctors because of medical conditions; I am referring to the illegal use of it. How can students study, perform, and compete on an optimum level while intoxicated? They cannot. As a result, they are forfeiting their future dreams and aspirations. Many students are graduating from high school and college unable to find or to keep jobs because employers are testing for drug usage. Even though man was given the gift of free will, it is not the will of God for man to be controlled by a substance.

BOYFRIEND/GIRLFRIEND CENTERED

Who has not been hyper-focused on a boyfriend or girlfriend at some point?

"Let's pretend that Brady centers his life on his girlfriend, Tasha. Now, watch the instability it creates in Brady.

TASHA'S ACTIONS	BRADY'S REACTION
Makes a rude comment:	"My day is ruined."
Flirts with Brady's best friend:	"I've been betrayed. I hate my friend."
Suggests they date other people:	"My life is over. You don't love me anymore."

The ironic thing is that the more you center your life on someone, the more unattractive you become to that person. How's that? First of all, if you are centered on someone, you are no longer hard to get. Second, it is irritating when someone builds their entire emotional life around you. Since their security comes from you and not from within themselves they always need to have those sickening "where do we stand" talks.

When I began dating my wife, one of the things that attracted me most was that she did not center her life on me. I will never forget the time she turned me down (with a smile and no apology) for a very important date. I loved it! She was her own person and had her own inner strength.

Her moods were independent of mine, making her more appealing.

A sure sign that a couple has become too centered on each other is when they are forever breaking up and getting back together. Although their relationship has deteriorated, their emotional lives and identities are so intertwined that they can never fully let go of each other.

Believe me, you'll be a better boyfriend or girlfriend if you're not centered on your partner. Independence is more attractive than dependence. Besides, centering life on another doesn't show that you love them, only that you're dependent on them."[2]

SCHOOL-CENTERED

Another struggle some teens have is the desire to become overly-focused on school. Here is an example from Sean Covey's book "The 7 Habits of Highly Effective Teens."

> '*I have been so ambitious and so school-centered that I haven't enjoyed my youth. It has not only been unhealthy for me but it's been selfish, because all I care about was me and my achievements.*
>
> *As a seventh grader I was already working as hard as a college student. I wanted to be a brain surgeon just because it was the hardest I could think of. I would get up at 6 every morning all through school and not go to bed before 2 a..m in order to achieve.*
>
> *I felt teachers and peers expected it of me. They would always be surprised if I didn't get perfect grades. My parents tried to loosen me up, but my own expectations were as great as that of teachers and peers.*
>
> *I realize now that I could have accomplished what I wanted without trying so hard, and I could have a good time doing it.*'

---

2   Sean Covey, *The 7 Habits of Highly Effective Teens* (New York, NY: Simon & Schuster New York 1998), 20-21.

"Our education is vital to our future and should be a top priority. But we must be careful not to allow Dean's Lists, GPA's, and AP courses take over our lives. School-centered teens often become so obsessed with getting good grades that they forget that the real purpose of school is to learn. As thousands of teens have proved, you can do extremely well in school and still maintain a healthy balance in life.

Thank goodness our worth isn't determined by our GPA's."[3]

PARENT-CENTERED

It's important to love, respect, and honor your parents, but you should not put their will above God's. Always look to God's Word as your ultimate source of guidance and wisdom. Always know that you are responsible for your own actions, no matter what your parents are like.

SPORTS-CENTERED

Many teenagers' and young adults' lives are sports-centered. The problem with this thinking is that many athletes are neglecting their education in hopes of playing a professional sport...and that's a tragedy. Let's crunch some numbers and research the reality of high school seniors playing college or professional sports. According to the NCAA, the estimated probability of competing in athletics beyond the high school interscholastic level is outlined below:

Men's Basketball

- Less than 1 in 35, or approximately 3.1%, of high school senior boys playing interscholastic basketball will go on to play men's basketball at a NCAA member institution.
- About 1 in 75, or approximately 1.2%, of NCAA male senior basketball players will get drafted by a National Basketball Association (NBA) team.
- Only 3 in 10,000, or approximately 0.03%, of high school senior boys playing interscholastic basketball will eventually be drafted by an NBA team.

Women's Basketball

- Approximately 3 in 100, or 3.5%, of high school senior girls playing

---

3   Ibid., 21-22.

interscholastic basketball will go on to play women's basketball at a NCAA member institution.

- Less than 1 in 100, or approximately 0.9%, of NCAA female senior basketball players will get drafted by a Women's National Basketball Association (WNBA) team.
- Only 1 in 5,000, or approximately 0.03%, of high school senior girls playing interscholastic basketball will eventually be drafted by a WNBA team.

Football

- About 1 in 17, or 5.8%, of all high school senior boys playing interscholastic football will go on to play football at a NCAA member institution.
- Approximately 1 in 50, or 1.7%, of NCAA senior football players will get drafted by a National Football League (NFL) team.
- Only 8 in 10,000, or 0.08%, of high school senior boys playing interscholastic football will eventually be drafted by an NFL team.

Baseball

- Approximately 3 in 50, or about 6.3%, of high school senior boys playing interscholastic baseball will go on to play men's baseball at a NCAA member institution.
- Approximately 9 in 100, or about 9.1%, of NCAA senior male baseball players will get drafted by a Major League Baseball (MLB) team.
- Approximately 1 in 200, or 0.44% of high school senior boys playing interscholastic baseball will eventually be drafted by an MLB team.

Men's Ice Hockey

- Approximately 11 in 100, or about 11%, of high school senior boys playing interscholastic ice hockey will go on to play men's ice hockey at a NCAA member institution.
- Only 1 in 27, or about 3.6% of NCAA senior male ice hockey players will get drafted by a National Hockey League (NHL) team.

Men's Soccer

- Less than 3 in 50, or about 5.6%, of high school senior boys playing interscholastic soccer will go on to play men's soccer at an NCAA member institution.

- Less than 1 in 50, or about 1.6%, of NCAA senior male soccer players will be drafted by a Major League Soccer (MLS) team.
- Approximately 1 in 1250, or about 0.07%, of high school senior boys playing interscholastic soccer will eventually be drafted by a MLS team.[4]

According to "The 11 Rarest Careers" list — professional athletes are fourth on the list. Similar to professional fashion models, professional athletes rely on their bodies as vessels for success. Professional athletes are active in the NFL, NHL, NBA, WNBA, MLB and MLS — and provide entertainment for millions of viewers by competing against teams and exhibiting physical aptitude. Most professional athletes have dedicated their lives to fine-tuning their athletic skills.

Why is this career so hard to come by? Statistically, a person has a better chance of getting struck by lightning, marrying a millionaire, or writing a New York Times best seller than becoming a professional athlete. According to the Bureau of Labor Statistics, there are 9,380 professional athletes. The chance of becoming a professional athlete is about 24,550 to 1.[5]

I was a free agent draft pick of the New Orleans Saints and a recent College Football Hall of Fame inductee. Then, I tore my ACL my senior year in college. As a result, I had to surrender my football dream during the third game of the season. 1983 was a recruiting class of a possible 30 or more freshman. At the end of 4 years less than 25 graduated, and only were 3 selected as a free agent. Although I was selected as a free agent, I thanked God I was graduating with a B.S. degree. The good news is I became a pastor, an educator, and, now, an author. Many of my peers went on to professional careers, in and outside of athletics.

Young people, the odds are in your favor of becoming an attorney, doctor, nurse, educator, author, professor, dentist, psychologist, carpenter, or nearly any other career than a becoming a professional athlete.

---

4   2010 The National Collegiate Athletic Association. "Estimated Probability of Competing in Athletics Beyond the High School interscholastic level." Clint Newlin. http://www.ncaa.org (November 13, 2010).

5   The Eleven Rarest Careers. Allie Gray. http://www.rasmussen.edu/student-life/blugs/careerservices/11-rarest-careers-By (November 13, 2010).

CHRIST-CENTERED

The Christ centered paradigms puts Jesus first in life, and it has you asking this question before making any key decisions: "What would Jesus say?" Josh McDowell says it best, "Our children and young people need models, people who demonstrates what a follower of Christ sounds and looks like."[6] "Being models to our children and young people doesn't mean being perfect. No one is absolutely perfect of course, but our kids do need to see in us living examples of what true followers of Christ are like."[7] When young people are Christ-centered, they are living with biblical principles that will shape their minds, bodies, and spirits, which will propel them to be victorious in every area of their lives. This paradigm is the only one that has never failed because it's built on Christ and His Word (1 Tim. 4:12-16).

REWARDS OF RIGHTEOUSNESS

Abraham was a recipient of God's righteousness according to (KJV, Genesis 15:6) because he" believed God; and He counted it to him for righteousness."It appears one pre-requisite for righteousness is to believe God, His Word and what it says about any situation. The term "righteousness" means being in a right relationship with God and His will." Daniel and friends trusted God and believed God, so he rewarded them for righteousness by giving them favor with the eunuch. The Lord rewards those who are earnestly devoted to him and recognize Him.[8] There is an old saying that I love to quote due to truth, "Only what you do for God will last." The concept is clear: God rewards those in right standing with Him.

6   Josh McDowell & David H. Bellis, *The Last Christian Generation* (Holiday, Florida: Green Key Books, 2006), 166.

7   Ibid., 167.

8   Donald C. Stamps, *The Full Life Study Bible KJV* (Grand Rapids, Michigan: Zondervan Publishing House), 29.

DISCUSSION QUESTIONS

1. Define cultural paradigm.

2. Is it necessarily bad to be school-centered? Examine and discuss this paradigm

3. Is it necessarily bad to be boyfriend/girlfriend-centered? Examine and discuss this paradigm

4. Is it necessarily bad to be sports-centered? Examine and discuss this paradigm

5. Why is the Christ-centered paradigm the best one?

6. What were the results of the ten day fast?

7. What is one purpose for being tested as Christians?

8. According to the NCAA, what are the statistical odds of playing in the NFL?

9. Discuss this claim: "You have a better chance of becoming a doctor, teacher, lawyer, engineer, or nearly any other profession than becoming a professional athlete." Do you agree or disagree? Explain your answer.

NOTES

CHAPTER 10

GOD GIVEN KNOWLEDGE AND SKILL

"To these four young men God gave knowledge and understanding of all kinds of literature and learning. And Daniel could understand visions and dreams of all kinds" (*NIV*, Daniel 1:17).

QUALIFICATIONS

God gave these four youths great abilities to learn: a spiritual education (understanding of scriptures and dreams), and Babylonian secular education (literature, the ability to acquire learning, communication skills, arts) and so much more. For students having difficulty learning math, social studies, English, science, literature, or any other subject in school, know that just like Daniel and friends, God gave them ability to learn. It does not mean they did not have difficulty learning. It means that God provides for His children regardless of need. Jesus said regarding the sparrows, "Not one of them will fall to the ground apart from your Father" (AMP, Matthew 10:29), and concerning human beings "even the hairs of your head all numbered" (Matt. 10:30). Child of God, you may currently be a "C" or "D" student who has the desire to be an "A" or "B" student. Know that the answer lies in Jesus. First, pray to God for wisdom, knowledge, and understanding in Jesus' name. Second, the Bible says: "So faith without works is dead also for as the body without the Spirit is dead (James 2:26). This verse means that you must put forth an effort to study, ask questions, and receive tutoring when available and have an understanding that nothing is impossible with God for you to attain the knowledge in your weak areas.

COOL FACT

Did you know that Hebrew is written and read from right to left?

"The emphasis in the remaining verses of this chapter lies in the progress and growth, especially in Daniel, in knowledge and understanding in literature and sciences of the Babylonians, and a special insight into every sort of vision and a dream. Remember, Daniel was soon to demonstrate the calling and gifts of a prophet. Daniel met the first qualification to become a prophet in his resolute purpose to be holy, undefiled, and separate from sin. The second qualification he met by giving himself diligently to his studies. But an important fact not be overlooked is that God gave them knowledge. Daniel's attainments were gifts from God. Daniel learned this for himself, and we must learn the same truths for ourselves. As we grow and progress in this Christian experience, let us never lose sight of the fact that all we have obtained has come from God. If ever we do become proud of our learning, then we have fallen into the snare with those of whom is written, 'knowledge puffeth up.' (1 Corinthians 8:1)[1]

"The wisdom and understanding in which God gave to Daniel was not merely the wisdom of this world, but knowledge of a discerning kind. There can be no doubt that he gathered much in the way of the superstitious practices of the Chaldeans, for in order to serve effectively the Babylonian government, it was necessary that he should be Instructed in the ways and wisdom of the Babylonians. But God gave to him the greater gift of discernment that divinely directed insight to distinguish things which differ, that enlightenment that comes from on high and which no man can achieve by his own strength or endeavor."[2]

Daniel 1:17 says: …"God gave them knowledge." Why is knowledge so important? The Bible provides many scriptural references that support the importance of knowledge. "A wise man is strong; yea, a man of knowledge increaseth strength" (Proverbs 24:5) is a verse of scripture that points to the correlation of knowledge and strength. More scriptures include: Proverbs 9:10 (The fear of the Lord is the beginning of wisdom

---

1   Lehman Strauss. *The Prophecies of Daniel*. 1st ed. (Grand Rapids, MI: Wm. B. Eardman's Publishing Company, 1969), 45-46.

2   Ibid., 46.

and the knowledge of the holy is understanding); 2 Peter 3:18 (But grow in grace, and in the knowledge of our Lord and Savior Jesus Christ; to Him be the glory both now and forever); and Hosea 4:6a (My people are destroyed for lack of knowledge); and many more.

There is an old saying: "knowledge is power." This kind of power has the ability to set you free from ignorance of self, the environment, laws, policies, etc. We must remember that

when we have knowledge of God we have the power to break negative stereotypes, opinions, statistics, "slave mentalities," and walk in our God-given freedom. Knowledge is power.

GOD HAS GIVEN THE CHURCH KNOWLEDGE AND SKILL IN ALL LEARNING AND WISDOM IN THE PRACTICAL SENSE

Josh McDowell introduces two educational models from his book, *The Last Christian Generation*, to the church. These models are explained in the following paragraphs:

THE HEBREW AND GREEK MODELS OF EDUCATION

"The Passover celebration has been repeated by Jewish families for centuries as a way of passing down to their children the story of the Exodus, the story of the God of redemption. But to Jewish families, the Passover Hagadah ("telling") is more than a Bible story of historical event. It is an expression of who they are, of where they have come from, and a depiction of a specific way of life, a way of being in the world, and pattern of acting and being Jewish. Through such celebrations, rituals, and retellings, Jewish people absorb not only theology — who God is and how to relate to him — but they also define their identity and underscore the reason for their lives and behavior.

Moses affirmed the process centuries ago when he declared:

> *"Hear, O Israel! The Lord is our God, the Lord alone. And you must love the Lord your God with all your heart, all your soul, and all your strength. And you must commit yourselves whole heartedly to these commands I am giving you today. Repeat*

them again and again to your children. Talk about them when you are at home and when you are away on a journey, when you are lying down and when you are getting up again. Tie them to your hands as a reminder, and wear them on your forehead. Write them on the doorposts of your house and on your gates." (*NLT*, *Deuteronomy 6:4-9)*[3]

"With these words, Moses was not only proclaiming the truth, he was calling for a 'lived-out' truth — a way of life. Moses called for God's people to both orthodoxy (right beliefs) and orthopraxy (right actions) in a way that tied the two things intrinsically together, making the truth an integrated, relational part of everyday life."[4]

"The Hebrew model of education is quite different....**The goal of the Hebrew model is not mere memorization of repeated facts; the goal (as Moses made clear) is to live-out the truth. In this approach, truth is designed to lead to transformation. Truth is the educational approach is to be learned by practicing it in real life. According to the Hebrew model, the student has not "learned" a thing when he or she can repeat it to the teacher; it is learned only when it is reflected in the student's life.** In this approach, the testing is in the living. The question becomes not whether the student has the information correctly stuffed into his or her head, but rather how has the truth transformed the student attitudinally and behaviorally?"[5]

COOL FACT

Hebrew spoken today is a modern version of the same language communicated over 2,500 years ago

Now that we have a basic understanding of the Hebrew model of education, let's explore the Greek model for learning. "You see, practically all of modern education, including that of most churches and Christian school, employs a form of teaching based on a Hellenistic model of education. Greeks shape much of how we

---

3   Josh McDowell and David H Bellis. *The Last Christian Generation.* Holiday, FL: Green Key Books, 2006.

4   Ibid., 93.

5   Ibid.

think today about education and disseminating information and truth. Essentially, this Hellenistic approach is to present a student with rational and logical constructs of information that he or she is required to "learn." To determine if the subject matter has in fact been learned, students are asked to regurgitate the information back to the teacher. This is called testing. If the student can accurately repeat the information, he or she passes the course, and the pupil has been taught."[6]

"The Hellenistic model is adequate, of course, in some areas. For example, certain mathematical or scientific facts are not intended to transform a person's life. However, when it comes to the truth about God and his ways, the Hellenistic model, which many have adopted as their teaching and preaching method in the church, is woefully inadequate. If we present Christianity as a world-view to be discussed, debated, and proven on a rational basis rather that a transformational basis, we will in all probably continue to see the lives of young people go unchanged. If we hope to reveal God for who He is to this generation and lead them to respond properly to Him, we must bring about both orthodoxy and orthopraxy, right teaching and right actions in our children and young people. (After all, that is what Moses commanded God's people to do!) Therefore, we must craft a way of imparting the faith to our children that is more like the Hebrew model than the Hellenistic model of education. We must develop a spiritual formation process that not only declares but also demonstrates truth that is continually lived out in relationship to God and others."[7]

"As a method of accomplishing this lived out method of learning, we are suggesting a way of introducing God to our young people that requires an interactive response. Rather than imparting them cold theological facts about God that they can learn with their heads, we must develop material that can be used to induce a relational response to who God is and what He does for us. The point of the process is not merely to stuff their heads but to change their lives. And that is what the God of

---

6   Ibid., 93-94.
7   Ibid., 94.

redemption, relationship, and restoration is all about!"[8]

As one can discern, the Hebrew model of education answers the following questions:

1. Why aren't church youth maturing in their faith, leaving church, and getting worse?
2. Why are youth leaders and pastors so outdated?
3. Why is the church not effective in the lives of our young people?
4. Why don't youth events change lives?
5. Why is involvement in youth ministry not enough?

The answer is found in one word, transformation. The verb "transform" renders metamorphosis — a change of form. "Transformation" is the present imperative tense rendering a command to change in the present on a continuous basis. The knowledge of transformation is found in — "And be not conformed to this world: but be ye transformed by the renewing of your mind, that ye may prove what is that good, and acceptable, and perfect, will of God" (KJV, Romans 12:2). Our young people must be "transformed" from a caterpillar to a butterfly in respects to their lifestyle; this is a command from God. In our schools, we memorize information, take tests, and pass tests just like the Greek model promotes. But in the Christian faith a student's test is life itself and once scripture is regurgitated to the youth leader/pastor and has successfully lived out the Word in their lives...they pass the test!

Wisdom, knowledge, and understanding are given when we seek God's way of doing things. The knowledge that the Bible is referring to is of God and of His Word. When a Child of God excels in wisdom, knowledge, and understanding, he/she excels in the Word of God; this will affect their areas of study in Math, Science, Social Studies, and English when a student applies themselves in diligent study.

As one can see the Greek Model of Education promotes a secular education without the spirituality to apply it in many cases. For example, a secular education can teach you about health and wellness of the body, but it can't teach you how to keep your temple (body) holy. The

---

8   Ibid., 94-95.

Hebrew Model of Education promotes living- out the truth, along with education with a passion.

EXCEL

To these four young men God gave knowledge and understanding of all kinds of literature and learning. And Daniel could understand visions and dreams of all kinds (NIV, Daniel 1:17).

COOL FACT

-Pastor Bill Hybels-
God's Four Answers
• *If the request is wrong,*
God says: **NO**
• *If the timing is wrong,*
God says: **SLOW**
• *If you are wrong,*
God says: **GROW**
• *But if the request is right,*
the timing is right,
and you are right,
God says: **GO**

"By concentrating upon spiritual values and resting full confidence in God; God who knows temporal needs would supply what was necessary." These needs range from material such as food, clothing, shelter, to immaterial needs like knowledge and love. But first seek to please God and understand and apply His Word to your life. If so you can be like Daniel and friends excelling in elementary, middle, high school, alternative, technical college, and university or wherever the Lord is leading you to your calling, purpose, or destination. In other words the same amount of time use for training in an individual sport or hobby should be used in studying and training outside of the classroom. For example, if a student athlete spends two hours a day, four days a week preparing for a game, how much more time should be spent reading and studying on weekends. The key word here is balance. Furthermore, think of something you do well like skateboarding, running, dancing or reading and the time that's spent doing it, if you can only apply the same tenacity in your classes, your grades will improve.

DISCUSSION QUESTIONS

1. What is the goal of the Hebrew Model of Education?
2. What is the goal of the Greek Model of Education?
3. Why is the Hebrew model of education preferred over the Greek model of education regarding transformation?
4. Define transformation. What is the Greek verb for transformation?
5. Explain Romans 12:2.

NOTES

CHAPTER 11

PUBLIC DISPLAY

"At the end of the time set by the king to bring them in, the chief official presented them to Nebuchadnezzar. The king talked with them, and he found none equal to Daniel, Hananiah, Mishael, and Azariah; so they entered the king's service" (NIV, Daniel 1:18-19).

This chapter is about how the Lord will allow of His children to be on public display to show for His glory with their talents and gifts, knowledge and understanding, and through their willingness to live holy. The word exhibit is defined as "a display or to show and to present to."[1] However, this is not done in a religious manner like the Pharisees and Sadducees had recorded in the Book of James, "One who thinks himself religiously observant but who cannot control the tongue will find religious observance worthless" (1:26-27). According to James, the religious observance God cares about is not in a cultic manner but an ethical matter, caring of the helpless of society. 1 Timothy 2:10 literally means "God-fearing or the sense of obedience to God's commands." Pharisaism, formalism, self-righteousness, and sanctimony are sects and states of mind in Judaism and Christianity that God disdains. Jesus discusses a "religious display" during his ministry on Earth, "And when thou prayest, thou shalt not be as the hypocrites are: for they love to pray standing in the synagogues and in the corners of the street, that they may be seen of men. Verily I say unto you, they have their reward" (KJV, Matthew 6:5). The problem here is that the "Pharisees loved to perform publicly, rather than making prayer a matter of intimate communication to God, the Pharisees had turned it into an act to be seen by men again, demonstrating their supposed righteousness."[2] There is nothing wrong

---

1   Webster's New Dictionary (See Bibliography)

2   John Walvoord and Roy B. Zuck. *The Bible Knowledge Commentary: New Testament.*(Grand Rapids, MI: Zondervan Publishing House, 1983), 32.

with praying openly, as long as prayer is between an individual and God.

Another form of religion is "Formalism." Jesus speaks about formalism in Matt. 23:23 — "Woe unto you, scribes and Pharisees, hypocrites! For ye pay tithe of mint and anise and cumin, and have omitted the weightier matters of the law, judgment, mercy, and faith: these ought ye to have done, and not to leave the other undone." Jesus was not saying tithing was unimportant; He was saying they were completely neglecting one area at the expense of the other. "They should have been doing both."

Another form of religion is "inconsistency in life." For example, Preaching and not practicing in Romans 2:21, "Thou therefore while teachest another, teachest thou not thyself? Thou that preaches a man should not steal, doest thou steal? (Gal. 2:14). These are some forms of the wrong religious displays and are prime examples of what we should not be repeating.

YOUNG MEN ON PUBLIC DISPLAY FOR GOD

In Daniel 1:18-19, King Nebuchadnezzar found none like Daniel and friends because they were showing forth the glory of God. Remember, according to history their ages roughly estimated in the early or late teens. These young men were dedicated, faithful, holy, uncompromising, flawed, but mature in believing that God is an Almighty God and He can do anything but fail. They were in the public eye as examples for young people, the world, and Satan that you can live for Jesus at an early age. Here is a list of teenagers on public display in the Old Testament of the Bible: Joseph, Samuel, David, and Uzzia just to name a few. According to Genesis 37:2, 6-9, Joseph (eleventh son of Jacob) was seventeen years old when the Lord revealed a prophetic dream to him. This dream demonstrated how he ruled over his family. Provided here is a fine example of how the Lord called young Samuel to follow Him:

I believe

God generally begins dealing with young people between the ages of 9 through 19 because of the decisions they're about to make in life.

"The boy Samuel ministered before the LORD under Eli. In those days the word of the LORD was rare; there were not many visions. One night Eli, whose eyes were becoming so weak that he could barely see, was lying down in his usual place. The lamp of God had not yet gone out, and Samuel was lying down in the temple of the LORD, where the ark of God was. Then the LORD called Samuel. Samuel answered, "Here I am." And he ran to Eli and said, "Here I am; you called me." But Eli said, "I did not call; go back and lie down." So he went and lay down.

Again the LORD called, "Samuel!" And Samuel got up and went to Eli and said, "Here I am; you called me." "My son," Eli said, "I did not call; go back and lie down." Now Samuel did not yet know the LORD: The word of the LORD had not yet been revealed to him. The LORD called Samuel a third time, and Samuel got up and went to Eli and said, "Here I am; you called me." Then Eli realized that the LORD was calling the boy. So Eli told Samuel, "Go and lie down, and if he calls you, say, 'Speak, LORD, for your servant is listening.' " So Samuel went and lay down in his place. The LORD came and stood there, calling as at the other times, "Samuel! Samuel!" Then Samuel said, "Speak, for your servant is listening." (NIV, 1 Samuel 3:1-10)

ENUNCIATE PLEASE

The Hebrew name for Samuel is (Shmuwel) sehm-oo-ale.

Samuel as a child received his first prophetic assignment from the Lord in 1 Samuel 3:1 and 11-14. We see that God's persistence and patience in calling the child Samuel reveals His own purpose, plan, and pursuits. The same God that called Samuel the child is calling you to His own purpose, plan, and pursuit.

It is also revealed in 1 Samuel 17:34-37 that David, the adolescent, stood before King Saul explaining to him that the Lord has delivered him out of "the paw of the lion, and out of the paw of the bear" and that the same Lord will deliver him out of the hand of the Philistine (Goliath). Saul's response is "go and the Lord be with thee." The result of this contest with the Giant is as follows:

"Meanwhile, the Philistine, with his shield bearer in front of him, kept coming closer to David. He looked David over and saw that he was only a boy, ruddy and handsome, and he despised him. He said to David, "Am I a dog, that you come at me with sticks?" And the Philistine cursed David by his gods. "Come here," he said, "and I'll give your flesh to the birds of the air and the beasts of the field!" David said to the Philistine, "You come against me with sword and spear and javelin, but I come against you in the name of the LORD Almighty, the God of the armies of Israel, whom you have defied. This day the LORD will hand you over to me, and I'll strike you down and cut off your head. Today I will give the carcasses of the Philistine army to the birds of the air and the beasts of the earth, and the whole world will know that there is a God in Israel. All those gathered here will know that it is not by sword or spear that the LORD saves; for the battle is the LORD's, and he will give all of you into our hands." As the Philistine moved closer to attack him, David ran quickly toward the battle line to meet him. Reaching into his bag and taking out a stone, he slung it and struck the Philistine on the forehead. The stone sank into his forehead, and he fell facedown on the ground. (NIV, 1 Samuel 17:41-49).

ENUNCIATE PLEASE

The Hebrew name for David is (Dâviyd).

ENUNCIATE PLEASE

The Hebrew name for Azariah (Âzaryâh) Az-ar-yaw

Young David is still remembered today for his bravery against Goliath and is even apart of Jesus' genealogy. King David put the Lord first in his youth and God gave him victory over the enemy.

In 2 Kings 14:21 and 15:2 scripture discloses Azariah was 16 years old when he became King of Judah. Also, 2 Kings 15:3 the Word of God reveals that the "King did that which was right in the sight of the Lord" and reigned for 52 years. **God isn't concerned with age,** for He is outside of time. The Lord is concerned with the heart of man.

The Book of Luke describes Jesus as a child and how He "grew, and waxed strong in spirit, filled wisdom: and the grace of God was upon Him." (KJV, 2:40). Yet, Luke 2:42 reveals that the boy Jesus was "in the temple, sitting in the midst of the doctors, both hearing them, and asking them questions." Also according to the Full Life Study Bible Luke 2:52, approximately 18 years of Jesus' life passed without comment.[3] What was His life like during these years? "From Matthew 13:55 and Mark 6:3 we learn that He grew up in a large family, that his father was a carpenter and that Jesus learned that trade. It seems likely that Joseph died before Jesus began His public ministry and that Jesus provided for His mother and younger brothers and sisters. The carpenter's trade included household repairs, furniture making, and construction of agricultural implements such as plows and yokes. During all these years He grew and developed both physically and spiritually according to God's will full conscience that God was His Father (verse 49)."[4]

ENUNCIATE PLEASE

The Greek name for Jesus is (Iēsous) ee-ay-sooce'.

Many children, teens, and young adults are convinced that Jesus can't grasp their struggles, temptations, familial conditions. In the above commentary, the majority of Bible scholars are in agreement that Joseph (Jesus' stepfather) possibly died before He began His ministry at 30 years old, which resulted in Jesus providing for His mother and siblings like many today in single family households. The Bible states:

> "For we have not a High Priest which can't be touched with the feeling of our infirmities; but was in all points tempted like as we are, yet without sin. Let us therefore come boldly unto the throne of grace that we may obtain mercy, and find grace to help in times of need." (KJV, Hebrews 4:15-16)

According to the Bible Knowledge Commentary, it is said that Jesus "never responded wrongly to any of his temptations (nor could

---

3   Donald C. Stamps, ed. *The Full Life Study Bible.* (Grand Rapids, MI: Zondervan Publishing House, 1992), 1526.

4   Ibid., 1526.

He, being God), yet as a man he could feel their reality (much as in immovable boulder can bear the brunt of a raging sea) and thus He is able to sympathize (*sympathesai*, lit., 'to feel or suffer with') with their and our weakness."[5] Christ feels and understands our issues and weaknesses in life whether it be good, bad, or ugly. Yet He has provided in verse 16 "grace and mercy" in a time of need through the outpouring of the Holy Spirit — the supernatural empowerment. God has not only displayed Joseph, Samuel, David, and Hosea for His glory, but He also included you and me.

The Book of 1 Peter says,

> But you are a chosen people, a royal priesthood, a holy nation, a people belonging to God, that you may declare praises of Him who called you out of darkness into his wonderful light. Once you were not a people, but now you are the people of God; once you had not received mercy, but now you have received mercy." (2:9).

Here we see that we ought to show praises to God because He has chosen us first, redeemed us, sanctified us and filled us with His precious gift of the Holy Spirit.

TROPHY

The Book of Job is considered one of the oldest books of the Bible and it is a great display of God's power in Job's life. Job is on exhibit even today for the entire world to see, demons to tremble, and for God to receive the glory.

It deals with mankind's most pressing problems: "the question of suffering and man's relationship with God. Job's experience billboards the truth that man's worship of God does not stem from a business contract, whereby he earns material rewards from God. Man's relationship to God is not a juridical arrangement in which He is obligated to reward man for every good act. Instead, man is to trust God, worship Him regardless

---

5   Walvoord, John and Roy B. Zuck. *The Bible Knowledge Commentary: New Testament.* (Grand Rapids, MI: Zondervan Publishing House, 1983), 790.

of his circumstances, and rely on the perfections of His character even when God's ways are not fully understood."[6]

"Misfortune does not mean He has forsaken His own. It does mean He has plans that the sufferer may know nothing of. A believer's unmerited tragedy may never be fully understood. Yet he can realize that God is in charge, that God still loves him and cares for him. This is what Job learned. His three denouncers said suffering's purpose is always discipline (punishment for wrongdoing); Job felt it was for destruction (thinking God was determined to destroy him); Elihu stressed that the aim is direction (to keep him from death). **But God had two purposes: Demonstration (that Satan's allegations were false) and development (of Job's spiritual insight).** Therefore to attack God, to malign Him, challenge Him, accuse Him, bait Him, or try to corner Him — all of which Job did — are out of the question for a believer. To criticize God's wisdom only shows ones own ignorance. The chasm between God and man leaves no place for pride and self sufficiency."[7]

ENUNCIATE PLEASE

The Hebrew name for Job is (Îyôwb) ee-yobe'.

"Job did not receive explanation regarding his problem; but he did come to a much deeper sense of the majesty and loving care of God. Thus he came to trust Him more fully knowing that His ways should not be challenged. Though often inexplicable and mysterious, God's plans are benevolent and beneficial."[8] The Job experience is one that will always be remembered. His undying will to continue to serve God in spite of the circumstance is the reason we use this story to help explain suffering, why God uses it, and the end result of persevering and keeping the faith. God restored all that was lost and revealed Himself in a way would have never thought possible.

---

6   Walvoord, John and Roy B. Zuck. *The Bible Knowledge Commentary: Old Testament.* (Grand Rapids, MI: Zondervan Publishing House, 1985), 776.

7   Ibid., 776.

8   Ibid., 776.

DISCUSSION QUESTIONS

1. What are the two forms of religion mentioned in the chapter?
2. Name a few bible characters that were on public display for God's glory.
3. Memorize 1 Peter 2:9.
4. Read the Book of Job and describe his experience.

NOTES

CHAPTER 12

10X'S BETTER

"And in all matters of wisdom and understanding, that the King inquired of them, he found them ten times better than all the magicians and astrologers that were in all his realm"
(KJV, Daniel 1:20).

After King Nebuchadnezzar thoroughly examined the four young men over a period of time, he found none that could compare to them. This included magicians, enchanters, sorcerers, astrologers, wise men and diviners. The word **magician** is defined as is one who possesses occult knowledge, a diviner, and astrologer.[1] The Book of Leviticus 19:31 says: Do not turn to mediums or seek out spirits, for you will be defiled by them. I am the Lord your God. Also, this includes magicians that practice witchcraft on television or at carnivals.

Enchanters mean to practice enchantments, a conjurer, an astrologer or those who offered incantations (ritual chanting).[2] This is a forbidden practice in the bible.

According to Deuteronomy 18:10-12,

> *There shall not be found among you any one that maketh his son or his daughter to pass through the fire, or that useth divination, or an observer of times, or an enchanter, or a witch, or a charmer, or a consulter with familiar spirits, or a wizard, or a necromancer. For all that do these things are an abomination unto the Lord: and because of these abominations the Lord thy God doth drive them out from before thee.*

---

1   Francis Brown, S. R. Driver, and Charles A Briggs. *The Brown-Driver-Briggs Hebrew and English Lexicon.* (Peabody, Massachusetts: Hendrickson Publishers, 2003) 355.

2   James Strong. *The New Strong's Expanded Exhaustive Concordance of the Bible.* (Nashville, TN: Thomas Nelson Publishers, 2001) 31.

Also, it includes séances and pornographic music with hidden messages revealed when played backwards by the artists that can't be detected with the naked ear.

Sorcerers practice magic, witchcraft, and casting spells.[3] This is a forbidden practice in the Bible. The Book of Malachi 3:5 says,

> *"And I will come near to you to judgment, and I will be a swift witness against the sorcerers, and against the adulterers, and against false swearers, against those that oppress the hireling in his wages, the widow, and the fatherless, and that turn aside he stranger from his right, and fear not me, saith the Lord of Hosts.*

Diviners are fortune tells and psychics. This practice is forbidden in the Bible. Jeremiah says in the Book of Jeremiah 29:8-9:

> *"For thus saith the Lord of Hosts, the God of Israel; Let not your prophets and your deviners, that be in the midst of you, deceive you, neither hearken to your dreams which ye caused to be dreamed. For they prophecy unto you in my name: I have not sent them saith the Lord."*

Also, this includes fortune telling in botanical shops, psychic hotline on TV, Online psychics and in the community, tarot cards, books that promote witchcraft, as well as fairs and carnivals for money.

Astrologers study the heavenly bodies as a means of predicting current and future events in your life. I would add to this list by including horoscopes. The Bible forbids this practice. As believers we don't look to the stars for guidance! This includes searching news papers or the internet for a horoscope reading in order to get guidance for the future... which happens to be forbidden. However we look for guidance from the one who created the stars, the Almighty God!

Horoscopes/Zodiac signs originate from Babylonian astronomy. A working definition of the word horoscope is provided for the masses on Wikipedia: "A horoscope is a chart or diagram representing the positions and angles at the time of an event, such as the moment of a person's birth. The word horoscope is derived from Greek words meaning "a look

---

3   Ibid., 138.

at the hours" (horoskopos, pl. horoskopoi, or market of the hour). It is used as a method of divination and forms the basis of the horoscopic traditions of astrology. However, no studies have shown any scientific support for the accuracy of horoscopes, and the methods used to make interpretations are, at best, pseudo-scientific. In common usage, horoscope often refers to an astrologer's interpretation, usually through a system of sun sign astrology or based on calendar significance of an even as in Chinese astrology." Scripture forbids this practice in Jeremiah 10:2, "Thus saith the Lord, learn not the way of the heathen, and be not dismayed at the signs of heaven; for the heathen are dismayed at them.

Daniel and his comrades were better because of God's grace upon them. There is both a practical and spiritual lesson here. First, the practical lesson is that they applied themselves to their studies. They probably completed their education in their late teens or early twenties using their natural intellectual talents/abilities in their classes. They were not waiting on some knowledge to fall from heaven or a quick fix scheme. They did it the old fashion way, "they learned it." The Book of II Timothy 2:15 reads, "Study to show thyself approve unto God, a workman that needed not be ashamed, rightly dividing the Word of Truth." The Greek verb for "rightly dividing" is *Orthotomeo-orthos* "to cut straight." It gives the idea of a surgeon, tentmaker, and lawyer; the idea of cutting or "dividing", scripture from scripture. For example, a person doesn't become a mathematician by reading a math book. Nor engineer, surgeon or historian by taking one or two courses at a Junior College. One must study, study, study. Once you have done all you can do, obviously the rest is up to God.

Second, the spiritual lesson in reference to Daniel is that a believers' extremity is the Lord's opportunity. Daniel and friends held positions of authority in Babylon, in which they had to be acquainted with their protocol, culture and religious practices. Here's the grace of God, while they were in Babylon, Babylon wasn't in them because God kept them and they trusted in Him. What a great testimony! They knew right from wrong, what was acceptable and what wasn't. God gave the Hebrews boys spiritual insight of a discerning kind while serving in Babylon along with the Law of Moses. Today as Christians we have that same grace to make us 10x's better. What was the grace of God that made them 10x's better? After careful study, it was revealed that Daniel and his friends were given the same knowledge and wisdom of Solomon. This God-given wisdom (*madda* [צדם] is the Hebrew noun) is only used in two books of the Bible: II Chronicles 1:10-12 and Daniel 1:17. In II Chronicles 1:7, God visits Solomon in the night and asks "What I shall give thee."

Solomon's response in II Chronicles 1:10-12 was,

> *Give me wisdom and knowledge, that I may lead this people, for who is able to govern this great people of yours?" God said to Solomon, "Since this is your heart's desire and you have not asked for wealth, riches or honor, nor for the death of your enemies, and since you have not asked for a long life but for wisdom and knowledge to govern my people over whom I have made you king, therefore wisdom and knowledge will be given you. And I will also give you wealth, riches and honor, such as no king who was before you ever had and none after you will have."*

Here we see Solomon's request for wisdom and knowledge was granted, but it didn't guarantee his faithfulness to God; that is an act of man's will. Yet Solomon is considered the wisest man ever walk on earth before Christ. In addition, we see the same *madda* (wisdom and knowledge) bestowed upon Daniel and his friends that surpassed Babylon's unholy wise men. The Book of Daniel 1:7 says, "As for these four children, God gave them knowledge and skill in all learning and wisdom: and Daniel had understanding in all visions and dreams." It is here we see that Daniel and comrades were victorious over Babylon's witches, warlocks, astrologers, wise men because of God-given wisdom and knowledge as well as God-given insight and understanding in all visions and dreams including King Nebuchadnezzar and of the Babylonian Empire.

THE SUPERNATURAL

With the growing influence of spiritual movies, sitcoms, and books, teenagers appear to be mesmerized by the thought of the supernatural. From the Wizard of Oz, "Bewitched," "Ghost Whisperer," "Sabrina,"

"The Craft," "Harry Potter" or "Teen Witch" and much more have fed a growing appetite among our young people that's out of control. According to a resent Barna Group Report titled Ministry to Mosaics: Teens and the Supernatural statistics in 2006 of 4000 teens surveyed across the United States the shocking truth[4]:

- "73% have engaged in occult activity beyond mere media exposure and horoscope usage
- 27% believe horoscopes are always true
- 35% have used a Ouija Board
- 35% have read occult books
- 26% have played games based on the occult or sorcery
- 10% have participated in a séance
- 7% have attempted casting spells, hexes or have attempted mixing a magic potion
- 30% have had their palm read
- 27% have had their fortune told
- 14% have witnessed psychic powers being used
- 9% have visited a medium or consulted a psychic"

This research has showed that our youth have a hunger and a thirst for something greater than themselves, which can be sum up as a quest for the truth. Our young people want to know the truth. For example, why was I created? Who's God? Does Jesus love me? Why do bad things happen to good people? How do I get closer to God? Why are teenagers attracted to the supernatural? There are a few reasons why teenagers are attracted to the supernatural. First, many of our teenagers think that witchcraft is the truth, because they don't know the truth. Here's an illustration about the truth, how do you know a fake dollar bill from real dollar bill? Simple, you spend time with the real thing, so when the fake comes along it doesn't look; feel or represent the "real deal." Jesus says "I am the way, the truth and the Life. No one comes to the Father except through Me." (KJV, John 14:6). Many of our youth are unable to fend off the influence of a popular secular culture. On the other hand

---

4   The Barna Research Group, *Ministry and Mosaics: Teens and the Supernatural* (2006).

Daniel and friends who were engaged by a Babylonian culture were prepared as youth by their parents who taught them the laws of Moses and to resist a wicked culture, or they could have been lured in as well. Parents, guardians, Sunday School teachers, pastors, youth pastors and the Church we have let young people down by failing to give them a Christian biblical worldview through teaching, guiding, counseling, preaching, nurturing, and listening to their silent screams for help. We have failed to scratch what makes this generations itch! So let's get back to the basics and with the love of Christ and equip our young people with apologetics, evangelism, missions, biblical languages, prayer, fasting and a relationship with Jesus Christ.

4 WAYS THE ENEMY TRIES TO DISCOURAGE
(*REVERSE THE CURSE IN YOUR LIFE*)[5]

1.   The scriptures say that Satan is the father of lies. Even though they are now outside of you, unclean spirits may still talk to you. Don't accept thoughts, ideas or guidance as coming from the Lord unless it lines up with Scripture, it gives you peace and is a part of normal Christian behavior. The Holy Spirit never contradicts the Bible, never creates chaos within us and never tells us to do strange things. Typical lies from the enemy's routine might sound like this: "You haven't been delivered;" "it wasn't real;" "it wasn't complete;" "you can't keep your freedom;" "the demons are still inside you;" or "God demands that you do such and such a thing or else." Don't believe it. Make your stand on the Word of God. *He whom the Son sets free is free indeed* (John 8:36).

2.   One meaning for the name "Satan" is "accuser." You may find yourself feeling guilty for having had unclean spirits or for your past sins. Remember that all your sins and failings are under the cleansing of Jesus' blood and God has put them out of memory. On the other hand you may be told that you're too weak to resist the Devil, you are failing God or you are just a "lousy" person generally. The trick behind these lies and the ones just discussed is getting you to focus on yourself instead of Jesus. No matter what we are or have been, Jesus is perfect and He loves us. Remember that your strength comes not from your own faithfulness but rather from your faithful Lord. But *I for*

---

5   Ibid., 121-122.

my part rely on your love, Yahweh; let my heart rejoice in your saving help (Psalms 13:5). Relax in God's full salvation for you. The name "Jesus" actually means "God-saves" and not "Man-must-save-himself."

3.   The enemy may try to intimidate you with demonstrations of his power. Don't be frightened if things seem to go wrong for you for a while or if some symptoms from before deliverance seem to reappear. Remember that if Satan was as powerful as he claims to be, he would have swept us all away a long time ago. The reason that we are still here is that his power is in fact very limited. There is only one all-powerful person and He is the same God, the Father of our Lord Jesus Christ, who sends us the Holy Spirit to dwell within us. In other words, we're on the winning side.

4.   You may find yourself tempted with old habits or behavior that doesn't fit in with the Christian life. The Devil has a way of making the old times seem rosy to us just like he tricked the Israelites in the desert into missing the "leeks and onions" that they had behind in Egypt. Of course Satan forgot to mention the misery and slavery that went along with those tasty onions. Don't become nostalgic about the past but keep your eyes on the future as you prepare to enter God's promised land for you. Jesus didn't come to take good things away from you but rather to bring you real life. *I came that they might have life and have it in abundance* (John 10:10). Put your trust in Jesus and you will have the desire of your heart (Psalm 37).

4 WAYS GOD WILL ENCOURAGE YOU
(*REVERSE THE CURSE IN YOUR LIFE*)[6]

1.   **Focus your attention on Jesus.** Jesus' Blood is the most powerful protection in the universe. Moreover, Jesus came to shed his very Blood because He loves you. Confess the fact that Jesus loves you and repeat the following prayer every morning both in your heart and aloud: "Lord, I cover my mind, emotions, body, soul and spirit with the precious Blood of Jesus." Talk to Jesus everyday, sharing the good things and the bad with him. You can be sure he will not leave you. *And they have conquered him by the blood of the Lamb and by the word of their testimony...*

---

6   Joan Hake Robie. *Reverse the Curse in Your Life.* (Lancaster, Pennsylvania: Starburst Publishers, 1991), 121.

(Revelation 12:11).

2. **Allow the Holy Spirit to have his way with you.** Pray in the Spirit for at least 15 minutes a day. Let the Holy Spirit show you negative attitudes, habits, feelings and behavior that need to be changed. The Holy Spirit is God's power given in order for you to become like Jesus. He will show you things through other people and through your experiences. *Pray all the time asking for what you need, praying in the Spirit on every possible occasion* (Ephesians 6:18). *But when the Spirit of Truth comes he will lead you to the complete truth, and he will tell you of things to come* (John 16:13).

3. **Immerse yourself in the Scriptures.** The Bible is the written Word of God. The Word of God is a living thing that works in us even when we may not understand or comprehend fully what we are reading. Read as much as you can but not less that five chapters from the New Testament Gospels each day. If, however, your mental state at present makes this impossible, then, until the Lord has healed your mind further, concentrate constantly repeating it yourself. Select verses that seem to apply to you. You may begin with some of the verses quoted in this chapter. *If you make my word your home you will indeed be my disciples, you will learn the truth and the truth will make you free* (John 8:31).

4. **Tell the Devil and his unclean spirits in Jesus' Name to go away and leave you alone.** Make it clear that you intend to follow Jesus no matter what. Above all, don't argue with the enemy and entertain his thoughts because you can't beat him that way. Instead, clear your mind by gently praising Jesus. *Resist the devil and he will flee from you* (James 4:7).

JUST DO IT!

You have been given a variety of examples of four godly teenagers living in a hostile culture with a wealth of potential being unleashed. You too can unleash the power of God in your life that's been lying dormant or locked up inside of you due to failures, disappointments, lies, missed opportunities or life struggles by simply letting go and allowing Christ be God in your life.

In closing, just like Daniel and comrades were victorious in Babylon, you too can be victorious in this modern-day Babylon! "Consider the life of

Abraham Lincoln. His story is one of the most dramatic examples of a man struggling to release the wealth of potential locked inside him:

> He lost his job in 1832.
>
> He was elected to the legislature in 1834.
>
> He suffered death of his sweetheart in 1834.
>
> He suffered a nervous breakdown in 1836.
>
> He was defeated for speaker of the State Legislature in 1838.
>
> He was defeated for nomination for Congress in 1843.
>
> He was elected to Congress in 1846.
>
> He was rejected for the position of land officer in 1849.
>
> He was defeated for the Senate in 1854.
>
> He was defeated for the nomination for vice-president of the United States in 1856.
>
> He again was defeated for the Senate in 1856.
>
> **He was elected president of the United States in 1860."**[7]

Please be informed:

I can do everything through Christ, who gives me strength.
Philippians 4:13

There is a giant taunting the church with obvious contempt, swagger and empty boasting for its youth. However, there are young people in this generation like David the shepherd boy and Daniel in Babylon running to meet this challenge not with rocks or sticks, but with Bible's in their hands and the truth in their hearts, standing face to face, toe to toe with this massive figure of a beast. They began uttering these words "Thou comest to me with a sword, and with a spear, and with a shield: but I come to thee in the name of the Lord of Hosts, the God of the armies of Israel, who thou hast defied." (1 Samuel 17:45) Christ is raising up an army of young people that will take on this challenge, and will not bow to Babylon's Table (world), nor tastes its delicacies. Stop, look, and listen the ground is shaking, buildings are rattling... "It's a bird, it's a plane; no it's a Youth Quake!"

---

7   Myles Munroe. *Understanding your Potential.* (Shippenburg, PA: Destiny Image).

DISCUSSION QUESTIONS

1. Define magician, enchanter, sorcerers, and witchcraft.
2. Are horoscopes biblical?
3. Explain Deuteronomy 18:10-12.
4. Name one way God can encourage you.
5. Name one way the enemy tries to discourage you.

NOTES

APPENDIX A

Q & A

QUESTION ❓

I'm a high school senior this year. I've been going to church for most of my life. And to be honest, I'm kind of bored with my faith. I try to read the Bible, but lately I've been getting nothing out of it. I'm just feeling kind of empty inside. Is there something wrong with me? I've heard that apathy is a sin.

Is this true? And if so, what do I do about it?

ANSWER ✔

What a fantastically honest letter! I admire you for saying what thousands of Christian teenagers are feeling at this exact moment. They agree with what they've been taught from the Bible. They acknowledge it's true. They just don't feel anything about it. Completely normal, especially for someone who has grown up going to Church.

No, it's not wrong to feel apathetic. Feelings come and go. Emotions can be caused by everything from stress to illness to too much sugar. But apathetic feelings can lead you into sin if you use them as an excuse to look for a little excitement in the wrong places and/or to get lazy in your conversation with God. In other words, don't accept your current feelings for long. Three ideas for fighting back:

One, check your life for real sin. If you've started to compromise by playing with sin, you will feel uninterested in your faith. Identify any recurring sin in your life. Confess it. And ask God to make your Christianity meaningful to you again.

Two, get in the game. God gave you a spiritual gift to use in your church.

Are you using it? My Christianity sprang to life at 19 when my youth pastor asked me to start teaching a Bible study for junior-highers. Not only did it force me to show that the Bible is real (for them and me), it helped me find my gift. You'll have a harder time being bored if you're doing what God built you for.

Finally, spend some time with non-Christians. After, 18 years of church and Christian school, I didn't really know any unsaved people. Then I went to college. Whoa. Suddenly, I was having discussions with people who didn't believe anything I did. It really forced me to look at everything I'd been taught. I finally understood why Christianity was such a big deal, and I learned to appreciate it in a new way.

Again, your feelings are normal, especially for a senior. Don't be afraid to shake your life up a little — just don't do it by giving up on your faith. Instead, try new things that will force you to trust God more than ever before.

APPENDIX B

HOT TOPICS

EATING DISORDERS

Do you ever secretly pig out and then force yourself to throw up everything you just ate? Do you ever starve yourself for days or even weeks because you think you're too fat?

If you answered yes to either of these questions (or if you have a friend who does these things), here are some facts you need to know.

UNCOMMON NAMES FOR COMMON PROBLEMS

If you participate in the "munch a bunch — lose your lunch" routine known as bulimia or the voluntary act of self-starvation called anorexia nervosa, you are not alone. Eating disorders usually strike during the teen years and affect millions. While the majority of the victims are female, about 10 percent are male.

Bulimia can involve the eating and vomiting process, the chewing and then spitting out of food, or binge eating followed by the excessive use of laxatives. Anorexia nervosa on the other hand involves voluntary self-starvation and rigid dieting habits. While eating disorders seem harmless, they are very serious. They cause an alarming number of deaths each year.

THE FRIGHTENING FEAR OF FAT

Why do people become victims of eating disorders? Among the probable causes are low self-esteem, misconceptions about appearance, perfectionism, and a distorted view of sexuality. If the media says that "thin is in," it must mean that "fat is failure." Consequently, thousands of young people are literally dying to be thin. While society has declared that a person's outward appearance dictates his or her worth, the

Bible declares that God looks at the heart (1 Samuel 16:7). God is far more concerned with your inner character than he is with your outer appearance (1 Peter 3:3-4).

OVERCOMING THE OBSESSION WITH OBESITY

If you are struggling with an eating disorder, you need to seek both God's help and the help of others. Consulting with your family doctor will ensure your physical safety. Seeking out another person — someone who will help you discover the reasons behind your eating problems — will provide the emotional support you need.

SUICIDE

HERE ARE THE CHILLING FACTS:

One out of every three American teenagers has contemplated suicide. The number of teenage suicides has more than tripled in the last ten years.

Christians are not immune. Regretfully, believers do commit suicide.

WHY?

Those who have attempted suicide citied many reasons, among them:
- Pressure to succeed and excel
- Confusing complexities of modern society
- Breakdown of the family
- Significant loss of another person
- Drug and alcohol abuse
- Sexual and verbal abuse
- Isolation and loneliness
- Depression

Most said they felt an overwhelming sense of helplessness or hopelessness and a desire to escape the tensions of life. Others attempted suicide in order to gain someone's attention or to manipulate or punish another person.

WHAT ABOUT OTHERS?

If you have a friend or relative who is extremely withdrawn and depressed, here are a few suggestions to help:

- Don't ignore the problem. Talk to them openly and willingly.
- Listen more than you talk.
- Don't judge. Give support.
- Don't argue.
- Do get help.

WHAT ABOUT YOURSELF?

If you are contemplating suicide or if thoughts of killing yourself are in your mind constantly, get help. Suicide is a very permanent answer to what is probably a temporary problem. Your negative feeling may not seem temporary, but hang on. Help is available so that you can face your problems and go forward to enjoy life.

MATERIALISM

We live in a material world where we are constantly confronted with new items and are told, "You've got to have this." Deep down we think, "If only I could drive this car (wear these clothes, have that device, live in such-and –such a house — take your pick), then I'd be happy." We think and act as though material goods will bring us the satisfaction we desire.

Is this the way believers in Christ should live? What does God say about possessions?

MATERIAL WEALTH IN THE BIBLE

By scanning the pages of Scripture, we find that many of the people used by God were wealthy (Abraham, David, Solomon, and Job). The Bible also acknowledges God as the source of wealth. He owns everything (Psalms 24:1), he gives wealth (Genesis 26:12-13; Deuteronomy 8:16-18), and he decides who will be rich or poor (1 Samuel 2:7). However, Paul carefully pointed out that "we brought nothing into the world, and we can take nothing out of it" (1Timothy 6:7). So, no matter how many possessions we might accumulate, we can't take them with us when we die.

JESUS AND MATERIAL

Jesus told his followers to store up treasures in heaven rather than treasures on earth. His reasoning was clear — worldly wealth is only temporary, while heavenly treasure is eternal (Matthew 6:19-21) and can never be lost.

Jesus understood that what we value in life will determine our direction in life. When we value earthy things and invest in them, our focus is on the material world. On the other hand, when we concentrate our time, energy and resources on eternal investments, we are more concerned with the things of God.

AS A FOLLOWER OF CHRIST:

- What possessions matter most to you?
- How would you react if you lost those possessions?
- Are you investing in what can be lost or in what will always last?

"For where your treasure is, there your heart will be also" (Matthew 6:21).

DATE RAPE

DATE AND RAPE

The terms just shouldn't go together. And yet, alarming numbers of people are going out on "friendly" dates and coming home as rape victims. Date rape is a huge problem that stems from two perversions:

A PERVERTED PURPOSE IN LIFE

For many, "having sex" has replaced "having relationships." Make no mistake: The Bible says that sex is important (Hebrews 13:4), but it is to take place in context of marriage and love, not lust and violence.

A PERVERTED VIEW OF OTHERS

The date rapist sees the date as a sexual object, someone to be used to satisfy physical desires without any real concern for the other person involved. Rape is a violent act of total selfishness.

Contrast this with how God views men and women — made in his image (Genesis 1:27) and deserving of respect (Philippians 2:3-4).

RAPE VERSUS LOVE

Forced sex has nothing to do with real love. In 2 Samuel 13 the Bible tells of a time when Amnon attempted to seduce his half- sister Tamar. When she refused, he raped her. What happened next is all too familiar in cases of forced sex. "Then Amnon hated her with intense hatred. In fact, he hated her more than he had loved her" (2 Samuel 13:15).

GETTING HELP

If you have been violated sexually, please ....talk to a trusted Christian adult — a parent, pastor or counselor. He or she will help determine what steps to take in regard to your attacker as well as find the help you need to deal with your pain.

If you have ever forced a date to have sex with you, you have committed date rape. Rape is a sin and a crime; it leaves long-lasting scars. Until you acknowledge what have done, you stand guilty before God. Don't delay a minute. Go to God and ask for his forgiveness. He will cast your sins to the bottom of the sea (Micah 7:19). Then ask forgiveness from the person you violated. And last but not least, seek help. A counselor can help you discover why you feel this temptation, and God will give you the strength to overcome in the future (Philippians 4:13).

HOMOSEXUALITY

In the last decade homosexuality has come out of the "closet." Homosexuals have their own communities, their own magazines and news papers, even their own churches. But if you think that it hasn't as yet touched your church, you're probably wrong. If you attend a church that has more than fifty members, chances are someone in your church is struggling with homosexuality. This issue is one that we as Christians need to face in a compassionate and straightforward manner.

THE FACTS

Opinions vary greatly on the causes behind homosexuality. Some people say it's purely a matter of genetic orientation. Others say it is purely a matter of choice. The past experiences of homosexuality do, however, reveal several consistent patterns. Most homosexuals had difficulty bonding with their parent of the same sex. Many experience some form of sexual abuse in the past. Rejection by their peers also impacted many homosexuals.

God's word speaks plainly on the issue of homosexual behavior. It condemns it in strong language: "Do not be deceived: Neither the sexual immoral nor idolaters... nor homosexual offenders... will inherit the king of God" (1 Corinthians 6:9-10; see also Leviticus 18:22; Romans 1:26-27).

THE HOPE

God's Word may condemn homosexual behavior as sin, but it doesn't leave the homosexual in that sin with no hope. Paul condemns homosexual behavior, as well as many other sinful acts, in 1 Corinthians 6:9-10. But then in verse 11 he moves on to say: "And that is what some of you were." Did you catch that? The writer Paul knew that some of the members of the Corinthian church were former homosexuals! But they were also "washed ... sanctified ... justified in the name of the Lord Jesus Christ and by the Spirit of our God."

CONCLUSION

If you or someone you know is struggling with homosexuality tendencies, don't give up. There is hope. God has promised "hope and a future" (Jeremiah 29:11) to every Christian.

REJECTION

HAVE YOU FELT THE STING OF REJECTION?

A good friend gives you the shoulder.

A family member turns away when you need help and support.

A boyfriend or girlfriend rejects you.

A person to whom you are witnessing laughs at your beliefs.

WHAT WOULD JESUS DO?

"Nazareth! Can anything good come from there?" (John 1:46). Many people asked that question when news spread that the long-awaited Messiah was a carpenter's son from Nazareth. Jesus was well-acquainted with rejection. Throughout his ministry and in the events leading up to his death, he confronted disbelief and scorn. But the ultimate rejection occurred when Jesus was on the cross. When God the Father turned away from his Son, Jesus cried, "My God, my God, why have you forsaken me?" (Matthew 27:46). Rejected, ignored, and cast off. The spotless lamb carried the weight of our sin alone.

WHAT WILL YOU DO?

From Jesus' example, you can see clearly how to handle rejection — you go on. Jesus knew God's plan, and he simply followed it. Even in his darkest moment, he chose to pay the price so that you would never have to know God's rejection.

Jesus knew that his message would be received by some, mocked by others. He knew that the truth of his message would eventually cause the ultimate form of rejection: his crucifixion. But he stayed the course, forgiving those who caused his death (Luke 23:24).

If you are sharing your faith with your friends or family and they reject the truth, don't become discouraged or bitter. If a friend turns away, don't hold a grudge. Do what Jesus did, forgive, and then go on.

MORE ABOUT REJECTION

Psalm 69:4-7; John 7:25-31; 2 Timothy 4:16

TEMPTATION

HAVE YOU EVER BEEN TEMPTED TO ...?

Lie to your parents to avoid getting in trouble?

Rent a movie you know shouldn't watch?

Go "all the way" with your boyfriend or girlfriend?

WHAT WOULD JESUS DO?

You may already know the story of Jesus being tempted by Satan (Matthew 4:1-11). Satan tempted Jesus three times, and each time Jesus responded by quoting Scripture. Let's take a closer look.

Many people know the Bible very well. But quoting Scripture and actually basing your actions on it can be two very different things. You probably know that pre-marital sex is wrong. You can find Bible verses to tell you so. But when the time comes and you are tempted, you must choose your way or God's way.

That's what Jesus did. Not only did he quote the words that "had been written," he acted on them. The words were firmly planted in his heart. He already knew what to do. By acting on Scripture, Jesus chose his Father's way.

WHAT WILL YOU DO?

You too have a choice. You can choose to do the "right thing" — the thing that pleases God. Even though your particular tempting situation may seem overwhelming, there is always a way out (1 Corinthians 10:13).

You will constantly encounter temptation. Luke 4:13 says that when Satan had finished tempting Jesus, he left him until an "opportune time." But as you read the Bible and learn to resist temptation, you will become stronger in those weak areas and better prepared to stand against temptation. You will be better prepared to ask."What would Jesus?" And then do it![1]

MORE ABOUT TEMPTATION

Matthew 26:41; 1 Timothy 6:9; James 1:13-15

BULLYING

HAVE YOU EVER BEEN BULLIED?

There are countless number of stories of teenagers been bullied by other

---

1 Wilkinson, Bruce H. *Youthwalk Devotional Bible*. Grand Rapids, MI: Zondervan, 1997.

teenagers. A story is told of a tenth grader being bullied by an eleventh grader for months. The tenth grader never told his family, but instead prayed about it. The very next day as the tenth grader brace himself as the bully approach, something miraculous happened the bully walked passed him as if he never saw him again. That tenth grader was me!

WHAT DOES THE BIBLE SAY ABOUT BULLYING?

Psalms 18:3 — "I will call upon the Lord, who is worthy to be praised: so shall I be saved from mine enemies".

Proverbs 24:16 — "For a just man falleth seven times, and riseth up again: but the wicked shall fall into mischief". This scripture speaks of the many trials, threats and calamities a believer goes through regardless of age, yet he/she is able to bounce back or rebound because of the sovereignty of Almighty God.

Isaiah 54:17 — "No weapon that is formed against thee shall prosper; and every tongue that shall rise against thee in judgment thou shalt condemn. This is the heritage of the servants of the Lord, and their righteousness is of me, saith the Lord".

Matthew 5:11 — "Blessed are ye, when men shall revile you, and persecute you, and shall say all manner of evil against you falsely, for my sake".

2 Timothy 1:7 — "For God hath not given us the spirit of fear; but power, and of love, and of a sound mind".

WHAT ARE CYBER BULLYING, STALKING AND HARASSMENT?

"The same things happen on the playground can also happen online. Cyber Bullying means being cruel to other kids online. This can include:
  • Pretending to be someone else and sending hurtful or embarrassing
  • Telling someone's secrets
  • Spreading rumors
  • Threats
  • Hate crimes, based on race, religion, appearance, or sexual orientation"

WHY IS IT DANGEROUS?

"Cyber bullying can cause low self-esteem, skipping school, depression and even suicide. Online threats can be more harmful than face-to-face bullying, because there's no escape. It can happen 24/7. Kids may be afraid to tell their parents, because they don't want their online access to be restricted."

WHAT CAN YOU DO?

This information is derived from these sites and some are provided and recommended for further information.

- stopcyberbullying.org
- www.thebeehive.org/internet-safety/keep-your-kids-and-family-safe/cyber-bullying-stalking-and-harassment
- http://www.ncpc.org/topics/cyberbullying/what-is-cyberbullying

CHURCH

IS IT NECESSARY TO ATTEND CHURCH?

This is a million dollar question! It's like asking a soldier after enlisting in the Army before going to war is it necessary to go thru boot camp. The purpose of boot camp is to learn the fundamentals of being a soldier. Likewise, the purpose of going to Church is to learn the basics of being a Christian, as well as ministry to God, believers, and the world.

In the Book of Hebrews 10:25 the Apostle Paul states: "Not forsaking the assembling of ourselves together, as the manner of some is; but exhorting one another: and so much the more, as ye see the day approaching". The verb "forsaking" is in the Greek present tense indicating action happening continuously in the present. It is in this verse Paul encourages his readers not to quit meeting together daily, as a few were doing. For example, when a believer discontinues going to Church on a regular basis. In a sense this is equivalent to desertions, missing in action (MIA) or temporary unaccounted for (TUF).

DAY APPROACHING

The Rapture is presented in Paul's first Letter to the Thessalonians.

"Brothers, we do not want you to be ignorant about those who fall asleep, or to grieve like the rest of men, who have no hope. We believe that Jesus died and rose again and so we believe that God will bring with Jesus those who have fallen asleep in him. According to the Lord's own word, we tell you that we who are still alive, who are left till the coming of the Lord, will certainly not precede those who have fallen asleep. For the Lord himself will come down from heaven, with a loud command, with the voice of the archangel and with the trumpet call of God, and the dead in Christ will rise first. After that, we who are still alive and are left will be caught up together with them in the clouds to meet the Lord in the air. And so we will be with the Lord forever. Therefore encourage each other with these words." (1 Thessalonians 4:13-18)

In verse 17, the English expression *"caught up"* in Greek the verb is harpazo, which means, *"to seize upon with force"* or *"snatch away."* Most people are familiar with the word Rapture, which doesn't appear in the English or Greek New Testament, for it is a Latin word. The Latin word for *"caught up"* is rapturo, from which comes the expression "Rapture." So at the Rapture, living Christian will be *"caught up"* in the air, translated or usher into the clouds, in a moment in time, to join the Lord in the air. In 1 Corinthians 15:51-52 the Apostle Paul had revealed a New Testament mystery, which is the Rapture of the Church, which wasn't revealed in the Old Testament. "Behold, I shew you a mystery; we shall not all sleep, but we shall be changed, in a moment, in the twinkling of an eye, at the last trump: for the trumpet shall sound, and the dead shall be raised incorruptible, and we shall be changed." It is in these verses the world will be shocked at the disappearance or the sudden removal of Christians throughout the world. Many people are asking the question what's next on God's timetable of events. The Rapture is next on God's prophetic calendar of events.

WE WILL NOT BOW TO BABYLON'S TABLE

BIBLIOGRAPHY

Barna Research Group, "Third Millennium Teens." Ventura, CA: The Barna Research Group, Ltd., 1999.

Barna Research Group, "Ministry and Mosaics: Teens and the Supernatural. 2006.

Butler, Trent C. ed. *Holman Bible Dictionary.* Nashville, TN: Holman Bible Publishers, 1991.

Covey, Sean. *The 7 Habits of Highly Effective Teens.* New York, NY: Simon & Schuster New York 1998.

Excerpts from *You're Not Ready to Have Sex If...*Copyright 1996 Journeyworks Publishing, Santa Cruz, CA. Reprinted with permission.

Gray, Allie. "The Eleven Rarest Careers". http://www.rasmussen.edu/student-life/blugs/careerservices/11-rarest-careers-By (accessed November 13, 2010).

Harttill, J. E. *Principles of Biblical Hermeneutics.* Grand Rapids, MI: Zondervan Publishing House, 1947.

Jordan, E. Bernard. *The Laws of Thinking.* USA: Hay House, Inc, 2006.

Keil, Carl Friedrich. *Biblical Commentary on the Book of Daniel.* Translated by M.G. Easton. Grand Rapids: Eardmans, 1955.

Keil, C.F. and F. Delirzsch. *Commentary on the Old Testament* Vol. 9. Peabody, Massachusetts: Hendrickson Publishers, 2001.

Lyon, Christopher. Zelos: Journal for Student Disciples—Romans: The Case for Faith, USA, 2002.

"Daniel Diet Foods" http://www.planetpace.com/?daniel-diet-foods (accessed November 6, 2010).

McDowell, Josh & David H. Bellis. *The Last Christian Generation.* Holiday, Florida: Green Key Books, 2006.

Morgan, G. Campbell. *Life Applications from Every Chapter of the Bible.* Grand Rapids, MI: Fleming H. Revell, 1994.

Morgan, Robert J. *Nelson's Complete Book of Short Stories, Illustrations, and Quotes.* Nashville, TN: Thomas Nelson Publishers, 2000.

Munroe, Myles. *Understanding your Potential.* Shippenburg, PA: Destiny Image.

Myers, David G. *Exploring Psychology,* 7th ed. Holland, MI: Worth Publishers, 2008.

Phillips, John and Jerry Vines. *Exploring the Book of Daniel.* Neptune, New Jersey: Loizeaux Brothers, 1999.

Robie, Joan Hake. *Reverse the Curse in Your Life.* Lancaster, Pennsylvania: Starburst Publishers, 1991.

Schultz, Daune P and Sydney Ellen Schultz. *Theories of Personality 9th ed.* Belmont, CA: Wadsworth, Cengage Learning, 2009.

Stamps, Donald C. ed. *The Full Life Study Bible.* Grand Rapids, MI: Zondervan Publishing House, 1992.

Strauss, Lehman. *The Prophecies of Daniel 1st ed.* Grand Rapids, MI: Wm. B Eardman's Publishing Company, 1969.

Strong, James. *Strong's Expanded Exhaustive Concordance of the Bible.* Thomas Nelson Publisher, Nashville, TN, 2001.

"Trouble Teen 101" http://www.troubledteen101.com. Copyright @ 2009 Trouble Teen 101-Help for Troubled Teen Issues.

Walvoord, John F. Daniel *The Key to Prophetic Revelation.* Chicago: Moody Press, 1971.

Walvoord, John F and Roy B. Zuck. *The Bible Knowledge Commentary on the Old Testament.* Grand Rapids, MI: Zondervan Publishers, 1985.

Walvoord, John and Roy B. Zuck. *The Bible Knowledge Commentary: New Testament.* Grand Rapids, MI: Zondervan Publishing House, 1983.

Wilkinson, Bruce H. *Youthwalk Devotional Bible.* Grand Rapids, MI: Zondervan, 1997.

Yeager, Selene. *The Doctors Book of Food Remedies,* ed. United States: Rodale, Inc., 1998.

2010 The National Collegiate Athletic Association. "Estimated Probability of Competing in Athletics Beyond the High School interscholastic level." Clint Newlin. http://www.ncaa.org (November 13, 2010).

www.oskarschindler.com Louis Bülow - Privacy ©2009-11

TESTIMONIALS

"Dr. Michael Rackley's book "We Will Not Bow to Babylon's Table"provides biblical based insights into keeping Christian youth focused on the truths of God's Word. In a day and age when so many are walking away from the faith, Dr. Rackley's book is a must read to help parents, schools, and churches motivate kids to remain committed to God's Word. This book has the potential to become the gold standard for making sure the next generation remains loyal to God and to His work on Earth."

DARRELL "COACH D" ANDREWS, CSP
National Acclaimed Speaker and Author of the Book
"How To Find YourPassion And Make A Living At It."
Certified Speaking Professional
America's Passion Coach
Toll-Free: 1-866-4-COACHD (426-2243)
www.coachdspeaks.com

"This book is really inspiring, and it will help children in the future. I enjoyed every bit of it!"

ANTONIO DIXON
Defensive Linemen for the Philadelphia Eagles

"Pastor Rackley, this book is an outstanding depiction of how God intend to use our youth as a means to build His Kingdom."

TONY LEE
Pastor-Teacher
Pillar of Truth Bible Church
Baltimore, Maryland

"We Will Not Bow to Babylon's Table is a must read for moms who long to rear their children according to the Word of God. They will find wise counsel and encouragement in this helpful book."

NEKEA WRIGHT
Mother of four

"I feel this book will teach youth, like me, to keep God first and to stay focused in school."

DASHAUN WRIGHT JR.
12 year old

"Dr. Rackley has done a fantastic job of exposing common teenage problems and revealing how we can deal with them! This book will give all an opportunity to understand the hardships the youth of today must overcome. I encourage this generation and even other generations to read this book."

ESTER ORTEGA
Nursing Student

"Dr. Rackley has done extensive research in the area of names and personalities and how they define us, and I believe that our young people will benefit greatly from this information. Dr. Rackley's background and expertise is clearly evident. We, as a society, can't overlook how our young people have placed such unimportance with names and how they classify themselves. Dr. Rackley's shows great insight and understanding that young people can relate to and gain positive knowledge from this book."

GUY HOLLIDAY
Recruiting Coordinator and Wide Receiver Coach
UTEP

TESTIMONIALS

"I have worked as an educator for twenty-two years with ages ranging from 6-16 as well as in adult education and in the federal prison system. Words speak volumes to young people when presented and posed in the proper format; this book did just that. I yearn and research for material that is not only thought-provoking for students, but for me as well. I found myself pausing to reflect, eager to read more, and thankful that God allowed Dr. Rackley to work "out-of-the-box" with his writing. What I found most profound are the quotes and their placement within the text. Dr. Rackley is a gifted and blessed writer with insights that will propel and prepare our youth for the future."

PAMELA L. WALKER
Educator

"Dr. Rackley thoroughly addresses the core issues plaguing this generation by uncovering the 'need behind the need'; a phrase that was coined during my days as a financial advisor to describe the root cause beyond symptoms."

Your Teammate in Christ,

WAVE ROBINSON
Multi-Area Director | Fellowship of Christian Athletes, Central Florida
140 N. Orlando Avenue, Suite 260 | Orlando, FL 32789
wrobinson@fca.org | 407-644-8292 office | 407-271-2145 cell | 407-644-8912 fax
www.centralfloridafca.org | The heart and soul in sports®

ABOUT THE AUTHOR

Dr. Michael L. Rackley has studied abroad in Israel and is a graduate from Louisiana Baptist University, South Florida Bible College & Theological Seminary and Cheyney University. He has been an Educator for twenty years and Bible Study teacher for at promise youth and young adults at Miami Job Corps Center. He was also the Founder and Senior Pastor of *Mighty Fortress of God Ministries Church* in Miramar, Florida for ten years and has a passion for the youth of this generation. He is now the Founder/President of A pro-Israel para-church ministry called *Sound the Shophar Ministries, Inc.* in West Palm Beach, FL whose aim is to evangelize, educate and equip youth, young adults, and the young-at-heart with the Gospel of Jesus Christ.

In 2008, Michael Rackley was inducted into the Cheyney University Football Hall of Fame, the oldest HBCU in the United States, and was selected as a free-agent for the New Orleans Saints Football team in 1988.

Dr. Rackley is married to Andrea Rackley and is a father of two beautiful daughters: Deborah and Anna Rackley. Furthermore, he cares for his dog, Napoleon, who he considers to be part of the family. His favorite activities include watching war movies, working out, watching football games, motivational speaking, and hanging out with family.

If you'd like the author to speak at engagements, conferences, or to give a keynote speech at an event, please feel free contact Dr. Michael L. Rackley on facebook (www.facebook.com/DrMichael Rackley) or email him at rackleydeb@yahoo.com.

FOR MORE INFORMATION, PHOTOS, AND VIDEOS, VISIT
WWW.FACEBOOK.COM/DRMICHAELRACKLEY